FRANK LLOYD WRIGHT

BY PETER BLAKE

PELICAN BOOK A607

FRANK LLOYD WRIGHT
ARCHITECTURE AND SPACE
BY PETER BLAKE

PENGUIN BOOKS

Penguin Books Inc, 7110 Ambassador Road, Baltimore, Maryland 21207
Penguin Books Ltd, Harmondsworth, Middlesex, England
Penguin Books Australia Ltd, Ringwood, Victoria, Australia

The Master Builders was originally published by Alfred A. Knopf Inc.
This Pelican edition, taken from *The Master Builders,* first published 1964 by
arrangement with Alfred A. Knopf Inc.
Reprinted 1965, 1968, 1969

Printed in the United States of America by Edwards Brothers, Inc.

Set in Monotype Times

FOR CHRISTINA CASEY, KATHY, BILLY, AND ELIZABETH

ACKNOWLEDGEMENTS

I am greatly indebted to several architectural historians who have published records of Frank Lloyd Wright's work over the years: the most significant of these records were published by Grant Manson and Henry-Russell Hitchcock, and I have found them more accurate, at times, than the wonderfully fanciful autobiographical sketches published by Mr Wright himself during his own lifetime. However, Mr Wright's *An Autobiography* remains the principal source for anyone seeking to understand his basic philosophical concepts, and I am most grateful to Mrs Wright for permitting me to quote from that autobiography.

During the last fifteen years of his life, I met Mr Wright on several (to me) memorable occasions. I believe that he considered me to be a member of the 'enemy camp' during most of those years; but if he did, he could not have been more generous with his words of encouragement. I am especially grateful for a long letter I received from him shortly before his death, a letter in which he seemed to recognize that it was possible to admire Wrightian principles without necessarily becoming a slave to Wrightian idiom.

So, in the end, I am principally indebted to Mr Wright himself. He never saw any part of this book, and would have hated most of it if he had; but whatever insights into organic architecture my text may contain were, of course, communicated to me through Mr Wright's works and words.

PETER BLAKE
New York, 1963

This is the third volume in a series of monographs on three masters of modern architecture. The first volume dealt with the life and work of the French architect, Le Corbusier; the second dealt with the German-born American, Ludwig Mies van der Rohe; and the present volume is concerned with the American architect, Frank Lloyd Wright.

Wright, who died in 1959, lived to be almost ninety years old; yet for most of his life he was out of tune with his time: he was much too avant-garde when he began to practise in and around Chicago in the last decade of the nineteenth century. And though his domestic work became more or less accepted around 1910, it took only another decade or so before the European avant-gardists began to make Wright's strangely Art Nouveau details look Victorian in the extreme. There was a brief period, in the late 1930s, when Wright caught up and produced recognizably 'modern' buildings; but even these, superficially, seemed at times embarrassing – stream-lined like a Chrysler 'Airflow' automobile, rather than angular and pure like the constructivist compositions being advanced in Europe.

And when Wright died, his last work was totally out of harmony with what the then avant-garde was trying to achieve: his forms and details were, once again, Art Nouveau; his compositions were anti-urban (in an urban civilization); his preoccupation was with rich-ness and voluptuous form (in a year that saw the New Brutalists become the latest spearhead of the avant-garde in architecture). In a word, Wright was a 'square'.

Despite all this, Frank Lloyd Wright was, in all probability, the most influential architect of his time. This was not because he was easy to copy, as Mies van der Rohe is; as a matter of fact, Wright was and is impossible to copy, and his many, depressing disciples all over the world have come about as close to Wright's genius as a necklace at Woolworth's comes to the brilliance of a necklace at Cartier's.

Still, it was and is possible to understand the lessons of Wright's work, and to translate his idiom into an idiom of one's own – *if* the translator is an artist in his own right. The spatial concepts developed by Wright in his earliest houses were never successfully adopted by anyone until Mies van der Rohe came along and translated them into his own personal idiom. The structural concepts demonstrated by Wright look pretentious when copied by diligent disciples; but in the hands of great engineers, like Candela or Nervi, these concepts have assumed new and brilliant forms.

So the work of Frank Lloyd Wright is one of the great treasures of architecture – one of its great resources. Much of it may remain untapped and unexplored for years to come, for it will take artists of equal standing to interpret Wright's work; but much of it has already passed into modern architecture, through the interpretation of other artists. This book is an attempt to facilitate such interpretation.

Wright's life was one of considerable pathos. He gained his philosophy in and from a rural America, only to live to see his country turn into an urban nation, and much of his philosophy become inapplicable. He was a radical when it counted, but he lived to see his own radicalism made even more radical abroad – and then sweep through the world of architecture and render him old-fashioned. He preached a better way of life and of architecture, only to find that the only ones who could understand him were the poets – and there were precious few of those, and fewer still willing to acknowledge their debt.

All this is true; and yet Wright's life might have been more tragic if he had found recognition and acceptance in the end. As it was, he died out of tune with the twentieth century as he had been out of tune with the nineteenth. Those were not the worst centuries to be out of tune with; in any case, he died with a challenge to all conformists, and leaving an inheritance to all poets of the future.

ONE

Frank Lloyd Wright was, very probably, the last of the true Americans. This is not intended to suggest that he was of Red Indian origin (which he wasn't) or that his ancestors came over on the *Mayflower* (which they didn't). It *is* intended to mean that Wright was the last great representative of all the things his country once stood for in the world when 'America' was still a radical concept, rather than a settled continent: a symbol of absolute, untrammelled freedom for every individual, of as little government as possible, of the end of class and caste, of unlimited and equal physical opportunities for the adventurous, of the absence of all prejudice (excepting prejudices in favour of anything new and bold), of the absence of form and formality, and, finally, a symbol of a society of many individuals living as individuals in individual settlements – not a society of masses living in giant cities.

When Wright was born in the 1860s, America was still, to some extent, that sort of miraculous place. Only a dozen years earlier Walt Whitman had published his first edition of *Leaves of Grass*; and though Whitman believed (just as Wright was to believe in his later years) that the American idea was being corrupted by all the things that had helped sterilize Western Europe, the very existence of Whitman and Thoreau and Emerson was evidence of the continuing strength of the fundamental, anarchic dream of a community of individuals.

To understand Wright's position in American history, it must be remembered that Emerson, Longfellow, Melville, and Whitman were still alive when Wright was born. Thoreau had died only half a dozen years earlier, at the age of forty-five. Tom Paine and Jefferson were as recent a memory to Wright's family as Theodore Roosevelt is to the present older generation of Americans. The American Civil War was barely over. America was being interpreted (and criticized) by the spokesmen of the romantic movement. Frank Lloyd Wright, the son of a Baptist preacher in Richland Center, Wisconsin, was born right into that movement and never left it until the day he died.

One of the many oddities about Wright is that the exact year of his birth is a little uncertain. During the last decades of his life Wright always gave 8 June 1869 as his birth date, but there is some evidence that he was actually born two years earlier. Why he should want to cheat the record by a mere two years is something of a mystery, unless he was, at one point, loath to admit to his real age and found himself stuck with that little white lie for the rest of his life. This is not at all unlikely, as Wright, who had the looks and talents of a spectacularly handsome matinée idol (or former matinée idol) during most of his life, was delightfully vain about his personal appearance and his youth. In his last dozen years or so he became more and more touchy about the photographic portraits that were published of him. He was particularly fond of one photograph showing him, at the age of eighty, astride an impressive charger; on the other hand, he strongly disapproved of the frontispiece used by the publishers of one of his last books, because the picture showed his hair to be quite long – a fact that (he claimed) made him look effeminate! Whenever he saw a copy of that book on a friend's shelf, he would quickly pull out a pencil and start blacking out the long hairline in the frontispiece picture.

These rather charming vanities were, perhaps, an important clue to Wright's personality. To the outside world he often seemed arrogant, strident, full of conceit. Yet, in all likelihood, these characteristics were little more than a 'front'. He was a country boy all his life: a country boy who had been sneered at as some sort of 'hick' when he first emerged from the Wisconsin hills; a country boy who had spent all his life defending the simple, hick-like things he had learned about in Wisconsin against the condescension and scorn of urban sophisticates. He was intensely conscious of his clothes (he learned to dress like a king), intensely conscious of what people thought and said of him, intensely conscious of and deeply hurt by what he considered to be the insults regularly hurled at him by the city slickers. Although he liked to make a good deal of noise whenever he emerged from the brush to put in a spectacular appearance on some Big City forum, it is very likely that the noise was really nothing more than an understandable defence against the hostility he fully expected to meet in the city.

To him, the city was evil incarnate – and growing more evil by leaps and bounds. When Wright was born, there were only 38,000,000 people in the United States; when he died, there were nearly 180,000,000. When he was born, only one-quarter of his fellow Americans lived in cities; when he died, almost three-quarters had moved into the big urban centres. Wright himself was a part of the minority that had not: after his death in April 1959 he was buried in Spring Green, Wisconsin, only a dozen miles or so from where he was born some ninety years earlier. It seems to have been almost a matter of principle with him that he never really left the place where he first saw the light of day.

Wright's parents were anything but ordinary: his father who, in all likelihood, was born in England, had been married once before and widowed. Some time after that, in Wisconsin, when he was nearly fifty, he met Anna Lloyd-Jones, who was almost twenty years his junior. They were married and had three children, Frank being the eldest. Shortly after the birth of their third child, the Wrights moved to Massachusetts, where they stayed until the boy was ten, at which time they returned to Wisconsin.

Wright's father was eccentric, to say the least. There had been a tradition of preaching in his family, and so he became a preacher too. But his real passion was music, and he literally inundated his home with music from morning till night. To make a living, he would sometimes preach, sometimes give music lessons, and never do either one of these things very profitably. When his son Frank was only fifteen years old, William Wright suddenly disappeared; he had decided to abandon his family, and neither his wife nor his children ever saw him again.

Unlike his father, Wright's mother was an extraordinarily strong personality. Although Wright used to describe much of his childhood by referring to life and work on Uncle Lloyd-Jones's farm, the truth is that both before and after his father disappeared young Frank was his mother's favourite and probably a pampered one at that. His mother, according to Wright, had been absolutely sure even before he was born that he would be a great architect; she had dominated his life from the earliest years through her preoccupation with certain educational theories and systems; and she had sacrificed a great deal to enable him to enter the University of Wisconsin as a student in civil engineering. Yet, although Wright was quite possibly pampered by his mother and endowed by her with an enduring arrogance, there is no indication that he was ever a spoiled weakling. Indeed, the very opposite is true; none the less, he *did* rather worry about the fact that his face looked a little womanly. When Wright died, Alistair Cooke, the broadcaster and American correspondent of the *Guardian*, said that Wright used to look 'like Merlin posing as Whistler's Mother. Indeed, there was always a curiously feminine grace about him,' Cooke continued. 'He looked ... like a matriarch of a pioneer family.' If Wright had been alive to read this charming and witty tribute, he might conceivably have punched Mr Cooke in the nose – or would have, at a younger and more pugnacious age.

Wright, of course, was anything but effeminate. But it was his strong-willed mother, rather than his erratic father, who governed his early life and left her imprint on the later years as well. Grant Manson, Wright's scholarly biographer, has recorded one incident in particular that formed the young man's life most decisively: when the Wright family was living, briefly, in Massachusetts, the parents took a trip to Philadelphia to see the Centennial exhibition being held there in 1876. Mrs Wright, who had long been interested in various educational theories, discovered at the exhibition a small display explaining the theories of the German progressive educator Friedrich Froebel, who had, before his death some twenty-five years earlier, succeeded in establishing a whole series of kindergartens throughout Germany. (Indeed, he invented the word 'kindergarten'.) His basic theory was that children should be taught through creative play to experience objects, colours, textures, causes, and effects. (In a sense, therefore, he had anticipated the famous Bauhaus introductory course by seventy years!) To supplement his theories, Froebel had developed several sets of toys – most of them simple, geometric blocks that children were encouraged to assemble in different ways – and these sets of blocks had also become available in the United States. Mrs Wright immediately became fascinated with these objects and the theories behind them; she began to read all she could about Froebel's ideas, got in touch with Froebelian teachers in New York and Boston, and, as it was too difficult to send Frank to the nearest Froebelian kindergarten (he was too old for that, in any case), she set up her own little Froebelian school for her son in her own home.

In later years Wright frequently acknowledged the great impression these games made upon him. Not only did they give him an immediate, tangible acquaintance with shapes of every sort, but they also introduced him to ways of ordering related elements into larger groups of forms. Froebel's notion was that children should be brought to relate his blocks and other devices in imaginative, but increasingly *planned* compositions, and he suggested that these compositions might form furniture, or complete buildings, or even small villages and towns. In any event, Wright found these blocks a wonderful medium through which to exercise his imagination: Froebel's basic units may have been rectangular blocks (which tended to add up to rectangular structures); but, beyond these blocks, there were games using folded and pleated paper, string, beads, spheres, and cones; and the young Frank Lloyd Wright found delight in all of these as well.

When the Wrights returned to Wisconsin to live in Madison, young Frank came under the influence of his uncle, James Lloyd-Jones, whose farm, located some thirty miles west of Madison, became a second home to him. There he spent a good deal of time every summer working hard and close to the soil. It was pretty rough going, but, despite the drudgery, he felt that working with nature and natural things brought him in touch with values that had changed very little throughout the history of mankind. Moreover, as he got to know life on the land more and more intimately, young Wright saw that nature was a wonderful teacher and had answers to many questions that theoretical learning could not explain nearly so well.

That is how young Frank Lloyd Wright grew up: largely dominated by an extraordinarily powerful mother who adored him and did everything possible to lead him to greatness; close to the wildly romantic traditions of his mother's pure Welsh ancestors (whose motto, 'Truth against the World', was both a defiant statement of rationalism against prejudice, and a typical *Sturm und Drang* slogan of a passionately individualistic era); and just as close to the land where his mother's forebears had worked and he, Frank, would also work and live and die. These are the names of near-by towns and villages: Lone Rock, Black Earth, Blue River. Spring Green was where Uncle James Lloyd-Jones had his farm. These names are part of the romance of Wright's life – part of what he took from the Wisconsin hills and tried to convey to the world at large as a great and lasting principle.

TWO

When William Wright walked out on his family, Frank decided that he had to go to work and help support his mother and his sisters. He was then only in his teens, but his preoccupation with building made it perfectly clear to him where to turn for work, and he took a job with a local contractor in Madison. As there were no architects in the town, Allen Conover, Wright's employer, designed as well as built his structures; and while their design was undistinguished, their construction was generally very solid.

Young Wright started as an apprentice to Conover and moved on to becoming supervisor of construction on several jobs. At the same time, he spent a few hours each day at the University of Wisconsin, studying civil engineering. After some two years of this combined study and apprenticeship, Wright left Conover's office, as well as the university, and went to Chicago. To fortify him, his mother (who strongly disapproved of the move) had given him a copy of Plutarch's *Lives*, and sewn a little mink collar on his tweed coat. Wright was no more than eighteen years old; he had spent less than two years in intermittent study at the university; he had had some apprenticeship in building; he had had no chance to acquire stylistic prejudices about architecture; and he had enormous confidence in his own ability. This confidence together with whatever genius he might be able to summon from within himself were his only tangible assets.

Going to Chicago was not as much a risk as it may appear in retrospect. One of Wright's uncles, the Reverend Jenkin Lloyd-Jones, had commissioned a well-known Chicago architect, Lyman Silsbee, to design a new church for his congregation. It was pretty well understood that young Frank could get a job in Silsbee's office to work on that church if he wanted to – and he did.

Wright stayed with Silsbee for less than a year, but the man's influence upon him was quite considerable. Silsbee, though an Easterner, had none of the growing infatuation with the neo-classicism being preached by the Beaux Arts Academy in Paris; instead, his own style was rather comfortably, informally English – a sort of early 'cottage style', somewhat rambling, soft, romantic, never ostentatious, always restrained. Silsbee liked to use many elements then in fashion: shingled walls, porches with archways leading into them, hexagonal rooms or bays jutting out of rooms, picturesque combinations of chimneys, dormers, and intersecting roof planes. Although there was nothing in the least bit unconventional about Silsbee, his ground rules, if any, were so flexible when compared with those of the neo-classicists that Wright was able to pick and choose from a fairly broad range of details, forms, and expressions. Silsbee was good for Wright, not only because he opened his eyes to a number of new possibilities, but also because he did not limit Wright's growth at a critical moment by forcing him into any stylistic strait jacket.

Wright left Silsbee's office late in 1887 to take a job with the firm of Adler & Sullivan. Louis H. Sullivan was then only beginning to make his mark, though architects and draughtsmen, especially in Chicago, knew that his approach differed radically from the accepted notions of polite architecture of the period. Sullivan had written and spoken of a new 'democratic' architecture whose form would develop naturally out of structure, material, and function. Although he was only in his early thirties when Wright came to him, Sullivan was already looked upon as the great white hope of Chicago architecture; and just before Wright walked into his office, Dankmar Adler and Louis Sullivan had won the commission to build the Chicago Auditorium, the great opera house which was supposed to establish Chicago as the cultural centre of the United States.

Although the sketches Wright showed to Sullivan when he came to ask for a job left the older man rather cold, Wright was hired and put to work on the Auditorium drawings. In those days Sullivan was still strongly influenced by the massive, Romanesque stone buildings of Henry Hobson Richardson, and the exterior of the Auditorium was to owe a great deal to Richardson's vigorous Marshall Field warehouse, almost completed at the time of Richardson's death in 1886. But inside, the Auditorium was a burst of exuberance and decorative delight that was strictly Sullivan's own characteristic ornament. This ornament, with which he liked to cover huge surfaces, consisted of intricately entwined plants – grasses and leaves forming a lacy pattern without beginning or end. Sullivan used to draw this ornament, free-hand and full-size, on endless rolls of paper which would then be turned over to the terracotta men or the plasterers to reproduce in three dimensions.

To work on the Auditorium was Wright's principal assignment in Adler & Sullivan's office for a year or more. It made an enormous impression upon him, and in many different ways. But most importantly, perhaps, the work on the Auditorium introduced Wright to what was, in effect, the vocabulary of Art Nouveau – for Sullivan's concept of ornament was, in most essentials, undistinguishable from the sort of thing done by William Morris and others in England and on the Continent. Like Sullivan, these artists tried to find a new 'honesty' in design, and they saw in the forms of nature a complete set of principles which, if followed, would inevitably lead to this new honesty in expression. The Art Nouveau movement was given added impetus by the newly discovered decorative work from Japan which was largely based upon forms in nature and had developed a highly stylized set of images based upon these forms.

Art Nouveau, in the hands of lesser men, tended to degenerate simply into another form of surface decoration. And surface decoration is indeed what Sullivan produced with his Art Nouveau designs. But both to him and, much more so, to his brilliant young assistant, the forms found in nature seemed to hold a deeper meaning; for these were, in effect, structural forms, though of a sort that Sullivan, at least, was never able to grasp in their full implication. He remained to the end interested in the rectangular cage, the more or less modular skyscraper frame that we have come to accept as a commonplace today. He realized (unlike many of his successors in the skyscraper game) that the proportion of a structural bay was all-important, and that changing the proportion as the building rose to its full height added an infinitely subtle touch to the drama of the soaring, vertical shaft. He also saw in his ornament (which really became an over-all texture whose detail was apparent only at very close quarters) a means of enriching the flat slabs his cagelike buildings must inevitably become.

All this Sullivan understood clearly, and he sensed, perhaps, that there was an inner meaning in the forms of plants, which he used as a basis of his ornament – an inner meaning that might lead to a very different kind of structure and architecture. But he only sensed it; it was Frank Lloyd Wright who, many years later, began to see through the tracery of Sullivan's ornament at the Auditorium and elsewhere, and saw through it a great architectural truth – a principle he was later to call 'organic architecture'.

When Wright first entered Adler & Sullivan's office, he found the going tough. He was considered something of an upstart by his fellow draughtsmen. They thought he was crude, uneducated, and arrogant. They ganged up on the country hick and made life hard for him from the first day on. In many respects Wright undoubtedly provoked whatever animosity he encountered in Sullivan's office. More than fifty years later, in his *Autobiography*, he recalled his first impressions of that office in less than appealing language. Here he is, describing the draftsmen in the Adler & Sullivan office:

To the right Eisendrath – apparently stupid. Jewish. Behind me to the left Ottenheimer – alert, apparently bright. Jew too. Turned around to survey the group. Isbell, Jew? Gaylord, no – not. Weydert, Jew undoubtedly. Directly behind, Weatherwax. Couldn't make him out. In the corner Andresen – Swedish. Several more Jewish faces. Of course – I thought, because Mr Adler himself must be a Jew. . . .

Finally, one day the animosity engendered by the cocky youngster from Wisconsin exploded into a fist fight. Wright recalls this too in his *Autobiography*:

I laid down my pencil, swung around on the stool and looked at him. He sat at his table, a heavy-bodied, short-legged, pompadoured, conceited, red-faced Jew, wearing gold glasses. . . . I got up and walked slowly over to him and without realizing he was wearing glasses, or hesitating, struck him square, full in the face with my right hand, knocking him from his stool to the floor, smashing his glasses. I might have blinded him. . . .

These passages from Wright's *Autobiography* sound as repellent as a Nazi tract; but the man who is speaking is a rather primitive countryman by instinct, and this includes the usual run-of-the-mill prejudices. Undoubtedly, to a Wisconsin farm boy, Jews were 'Big City' crooks, and had to be handled accordingly. Many years later, when Wright had his Fellowship of young apprentices in Wisconsin and Arizona, he demonstrated again and again – and not publicly at any time – his utter lack of prejudice in the conventional areas of race, colour, and creed. Indeed, it almost seems as if he included these faintly nauseating paragraphs in his *Autobiography* as an act of penance; for even while he was writing these sentences, he was busy demonstrating, by his private actions, that he had no hatred for anything in life except cruelty and sham.

Wright won his fist fight in Sullivan's office, and soon after he was accepted as an equal by the men in the draughting room. The fact that Sullivan saw great promise in the young man naturally helped: within two years after Wright had joined the firm, he was given his own private office next door to Sullivan's. By this time Wright was just twenty-one years old, but Sullivan had seen in him so great a talent that he was willing to turn over to this young man an increasing amount of work and responsibility.

Like many architectural offices doing large buildings, Adler & Sullivan were not properly organized to take on the design of private houses. However, there were frequent occasions when an important businessman-client asked to have a house designed for his own family, and the firm could not afford to turn him down. These jobs were handed to Wright, who, in turn, did most of the drawings at home in his spare time and only occasionally brought his designs to Sullivan for criticism. This arrangement became so routine that Wright was, in effect, almost solely responsible for all domestic work in Adler & Sullivan's offices from about 1888 on. These houses represent Wright's earliest independent work, and one of them – the Charnley house, built in 1891 – revealed Wright's independent genius for the first time.

The Charnley house had many extraordinary facets, but in retrospect its most important characteristic is its extreme 'modernity' – a kind of modernity which was not to be emulated by the pioneer European architects until twenty or thirty years later. For the Charnley house was an entirely smooth, geometric block, three storeys high, rendered in precise brickwork (Wright used a flat, elongated brick, known as 'Roman brick' to the trade), and composed in an absolutely classical, symmetrical way. The windows were unadorned rectangles cut out of the masonry wall, and the roof appeared to be a thin, flat slab projecting out beyond the face of the building. The composition was severe in the classical manner: there was a base, a truncated masonry shaft, and then the slab roof. (Sullivan, who treated his skyscrapers much as the Greeks and Romans handled a column, generally used a base, a shaft, and a projecting roof-cap to balance his tall buildings.) In short, the Charnley house was Wright's first completely disciplined and unromantic statement. When he attacked the International Style architects in later years and criticized the boxiness of their buildings, he liked to mention, casually, that he had done *his* box a few decades earlier and had grown out of it. The Charnley house was that box.

As a matter of fact, the house did show certain romantic, Art Nouveau touches, which Wright had obviously acquired from Sullivan. Over the main entrance door there was a projecting balcony, whose parapet was ornamented in a typically Sullivanesque manner; and the edge of the flat, projecting roof was decorated with a continuous frieze that is reminiscent of Sullivan's decorative treatment of the roof fascia of the Wainwright building in St Louis, completed in 1890 while Wright was working in the Adler & Sullivan office. Wright was never able completely to throw off the delight in ornamentation which he acquired from Sullivan; and this fact, more than any other, made him often seem old-fashioned in later years. Actually, the ornament on the Charnley house was extremely graceful, whereas much of Wright's later applied ornament on roof fascias and wall panels became embarrassingly crude and even 'jazzy'. The reason may have been that Wright tried to modernize what he had learned from Sullivan in the field of decoration, rather than copy it or give it up entirely. However that may be, the decorative friezes on the Charnley house are among the best Wright ever achieved.

Inside, the Charnley house was just as simple as its elevations suggested. Yet it was still very definitely 'inside'; there was none of the interpenetration of interior and exterior spaces which Wright learned to handle to such perfection in later years. However, many of his later details are first suggested in these interiors, particularly the use of strong, linear, horizontal bands that create distinct levels within rooms and along walls. Except for a profusion of ornament in a few scattered areas, the Charnley house interiors were as simple as anything done by the Austrian pioneer Adolf Loos and others twenty years later.

While Wright was doing Adler & Sullivan's houses in his spare time, he spent the days working on some of the large projects then in the office. Among these the most important one was the Transportation building for the World's Columbian exhibition held in Chicago in 1893.

The Chicago Fair, as a whole, has been described by Wright and others as a serious setback to the independent architectural movement just getting under way in Chicago. For various complex political reasons, the Chicago Fair was turned over almost in its entirety to the Eastern architects who represented the neo-classicist party line of the Beaux Arts. This fact did, indeed, constitute a severe blow to

Sullivan and a few others who had broken away from the snobbish 'upper-class' architecture being imported from Europe, and had tried to create a genuinely American, 'democratic' expression. What Sullivan meant by this was never made completely clear by him, though Wright made it abundantly clear later in his own words and works. Basically, the conflict lay between the Beaux Arts men on the one hand, who could forget architectural 'honesty' and apply false fronts designed according to preconceived, neo-classical standards to any building regardless of its function; and those like Sullivan and Wright on the other hand, who believed that 'honesty' was a function of function – that no building could be true to itself, that no building could be a true expression of the aspirations of those who built it, unless its exteriors clearly declared its purpose.

Sullivan was severely hurt by the rejection of 'democratic' architecture and the espousal of 'autocratic' neo-classicism at the Chicago Fair. The Transportation building, which he was asked to design, was located on the edge of the fair-grounds, the central areas being occupied entirely by neo-classical palaces of equal cornice height (sixty feet) and related arcades. These same rules applied to the Transportation building as well, so that Sullivan could not really make this an honestly expressive structure either. But in applying the great monumental front with its huge archway to the steel-framed exhibition hall at the back of that front, Sullivan and Wright tried to make a statement about the potential power and verve of 'honest' architecture which would be unmistakable even though it was only a symbolic act rather than a true architectural solution as they saw it.

They made their statement in two ways: first, they substituted for the colonnades of the Beaux Arts a huge arch reminiscent of Richardson's Romanesque arches, but rendered in lacy, decorated terracotta rather than massive stone. The decoration was, again, a collection of natural forms, intertwined in the Auditorium manner. To Sullivan and to his young disciple, the symbolic images of nature began, more and more, to represent images of America and of democracy as well. America was space and landscape – Europe was crowding and formal urban life. . . . The ornaments on the Transportation building were symbols of honesty, of down-to-earthness, just as Mies van der Rohe's steel pilasters of fifty years later were to become symbols of order and technological progress.

The second aspect of the Transportation building which made it distinctly different from its Beaux Arts neighbours had to do with its dominant line – the horizontal. The dominant line of classicism (and neo-classicism) is the vertical, the image of man standing up against nature. The dominant line of Sullivan's and Wright's down-to-earth architecture was the horizontal, the image of man in love with nature. If these images seem too mystical, it should be remembered that both Sullivan and Wright were mystics; and, indeed, Wright's mysticism was to become more and more dominant as he developed further his basic principles.

The horizontals that characterized the Transportation building were slabs and planes somewhat in conflict with the great Richardsonian arch of the main entrance. Indeed, it is possible to isolate, on this single façade, the elements that were contributed by Sullivan and those contributed by Wright. Still, the ensemble was splendid – the only building of the great Columbian exhibition still remembered by anyone today.

It has long been argued as to whether Sullivan largely directed Wright, or whether Wright influenced his first, true, and only master. There is little point in speculating upon the exact degrees of influence: without Sullivan, Wright could not have achieved half of what he did achieve; Sullivan was his springboard. Yet, without Wright, Sullivan, in later years, created nothing that went very far beyond the Auditorium, the Wainwright building, and the Transportation building. In short, theirs was a near-perfect association as long as it lasted; and the Transportation building, more than any other structure they designed together, was evidence both of the rich vocabulary Sullivan could supply and of the dynamism and verve his young disciple injected into the master's work.

THREE

A few months after Frank Lloyd Wright arrived in Chicago, his mother moved down from Madison to join him. Their means were very modest and they had to live in small furnished rooms. A year or so later, mother and son moved to Oak Park, a suburb of Chicago, to live with a friend of Mrs Wright's. Meanwhile, Frank had fallen in love, and by 1889 he was engaged to be married to Catherine Tobin, a nineteen-year-old girl he had met at a church social. His mother was opposed to the idea in view of their youth; but, by this time, Wright had attained so considerable a standing in the offices of Adler & Sullivan that they were willing to give him a five-year contract under which he could draw upon funds ahead of time to enable him to start a family and build his own house. So, in 1890, he and Catherine were married.

Their first house in Oak Park was quite small and looked, from the outside, not very different from the pleasantly shingled cottages Wright had seen in Silsbee's office. However, in several respects the house differed radically from Silsbee's polite 'cottage style'. To start with, it was much simpler, much less rambling than a Silsbee house; indeed, it was rather severe by comparison. Next, the Oak Park house showed a sense of interior organization which had nothing to do with Silsbee s rather unimaginative plans. There were few doors between rooms on the main floor; instead, adjoining spaces were allowed to merge into a single, continuous space modulated by more-or-less free-standing partitions. At the level of a normal door head (approximately seven feet above the floor), Wright carried a continuous band all around the walls of the rooms. All openings in the walls were kept below this band; above it was an additional height of wall treated rather like a frieze, and then came the second horizontal line, the ceiling. This little detail is one that Wright perfected and made an essential part of his vocabulary in later years. It is an extremely helpful device of spatial organization, for the lower horizontal band at door level brings the height of any room down to the scale of the human figure, without, at the same time, making the ceiling itself oppressively low. (The standard door height of seven feet corresponds roughly to the height of a man standing with upraised arm – the basic Modulor figure that Le Corbusier was to adopt as the point of departure for his proportionate scale some fifty years later!)

Finally, the little Oak Park house contained various details that were either 'Sullivanesque' or, for the first time, originally 'Wrightian'. There was a brick fireplace with an arched opening reminiscent of Richardson's and Sullivan's great arches; there were decorative friezes (though only a very few of them) not unlike Sullivan's; and there was the hint of an important idea that Wright was to perfect in years to come: the idea of the 'utility core', a central, compact arrangement of fireplace and kitchen, back to back. This was, of course, a standard feature of every Cape Cod house; but in Wright's vocabulary this core became not only a central-heating system, but a sort of mystical life-giving element in the heart of his houses, from which all spaces expanded and radiated towards a distant horizon. The Oak Park house had none of this drama – or, for that matter, the setting necessary for such a dramatic composition. But even this small project contained the seed of Wright's later powerful radial plans.

Under Wright's contract with Adler & Sullivan, he was expected to continue to do the firm's residential work in his spare time. As this domestic practice grew, people began to come to Wright directly, and he designed a number of private houses on the sly, sometimes using a pseudonym to hide the fact from Sullivan. These 'bootlegged' houses, as he called them, may, in retrospect, seem to have involved some sort of breach of faith on his part; however, the chances are that these commissions started to come to him directly in a rather casual way, and, as Sullivan was not particularly interested in such work, Wright probably did not want to bother him with it. Soon, however, the houses began to take up an increasing amount of Wright's time, and, as he was always short of cash (a chronic state of affairs throughout his life), he welcomed the chance to increase his income. He was obviously embarrassed by the subterfuge all this involved, but he was soon too deeply involved in this clandestine practice to extricate himself. One day in 1893 Sullivan discovered what Wright had been up to. There was a terrible row, and Wright walked out of Adler & Sullivan's offices. He did not see Sullivan again until many years later.

The only influence on his work which Wright ever acknowledged was that of Louis Sullivan. Yet it seems, in retrospect, as if it was Sullivan's *idea*, rather than Sullivan's actual work, that gave Wright some of the impetus he needed. Sullivan's notion, poetically expressed in many writings, such as his famous *Kindergarten Chats*, was that American democracy could not be built upon pretence, that a democratic architecture must be an honest architecture in the sense that it must express its contents and intents on the face and in all details of its buildings. Yet Sullivan never for a moment believed that buildings which expressed their structure and their function must therefore, inevitably, be beautiful. All he did believe was that honesty of expression was the ethical basis of a democratic architecture – the only basis upon which things of true beauty could be built. His dictum – 'form follows function' – has been one of the most widely misunderstood statements of aesthetic principle of all time: what he meant was *not* – or not *only* – that form must grow out of function, but that form, *beautiful* form, could only be created after functional expression had been satisfied. In one of the dialogues between THE MASTER and THE STUDENT in his *Kindergarten Chats*, Sullivan wrote:

THE MASTER: I am endeavouring to impress upon you the simple truth . . of the subjective possibilities of objective things. In short, to clarify for you the origin and power of beauty: to let you see that it is resident in function and form.
THE STUDENT: So is ugliness, isn't it?
THE MASTER: To be sure. . . .

Here is the crux of the matter: when Wright, in later years, attacked the functionalists and declared that they had misunderstood Sullivan and him, he meant that the functionalists had taken the wrong turn at the fork in the road, where there appeared at least two alternative 'subjective possibilities of objective things'. To Sullivan and to Wright, beauty was only '*resident*' in function and form. It was never the inevitable by-product of function and form.

Wright was deeply attached to Sullivan, to whom he always referred as the '*Lieber Meister*', a touching if not quite idiomatically correct appellation. Yet there is good reason to think that Wright's affection for Sullivan was caused as much by Sullivan's paternalistic attitude towards his young disciple (who was happy to find a father substitute) as it was by any great revelation of architectural truths

2. *Wright's presentation drawing of a house built during the first decade of the century. Even the graphic technique is reminiscent of Japanese prints. (Courtesy, Taliesin Fellowship)*

supplied by the master. Sullivan's buildings were, without doubt, the finest of the Chicago School; they had a strength and beauty unequalled by any of his contemporaries. Yet the greatness of Sullivan's Wainwright building in St Louis and his Guaranty building in Buffalo lay in an ordered structural rhythm that Wright himself did not emulate for very long. Curiously it was Mies, rather than Wright, who learned the lessons of Sullivan's skyscrapers; Wright received from Sullivan a great idea and a hint of truths to be learned from things in nature. He did not receive from his '*Lieber Meister*' any important formal architectural concepts.

Sullivan's emotional break with Wright was perhaps as much the former's fault as it was the result of Wright's 'bootlegging' activities. Before long, Sullivan was to become a hopeless alcoholic, and the weaknesses that finally caused this disease – a disease that, in the end, brought him poverty and a lonely death – were apparent even in the early days when Wright worked for him. In any event, though Wright felt intensely unhappy and somewhat guilty about the break with Sullivan, he never ceased to honour this great man to the very end.

During the months of the Chicago exhibition of 1893, Wright saw on the exhibition grounds a model of a traditional wooden Japanese temple, reproduced at half its full size. This was the official Japanese contribution to the fair. Wright was intrigued. He had become quite familiar with the Japanese prints that were such an important source of Art Nouveau ornament [2], but this was probably his first direct contact with Japanese architecture in the flesh. For some reason he always denied, quite furiously, that there was any influence of Japanese architecture upon his work at all: but this is obvious nonsense; he was much more strongly influenced by Katsura Palace than by the Auditorium, and only his increasing arrogance could obscure the fact to his own eyes.

The black wood posts and beams, the deep roof overhangs, the white plaster panels between the darkened framework, and the intimate relation of house and nature – all these made a profound and lasting impression upon Wright. So did the open spaces within, lightly divided by sliding screens and separated from the gardens by

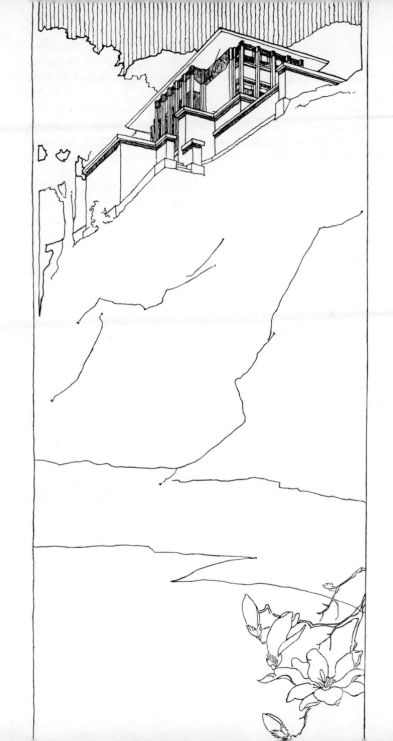

still more transparent and translucent sliding panels. And so did the strong, modular organization of the buildings, the horizontal emphasis (the door-height horizontal that Wright used at Oak Park had long been a standard Japanese device). Indeed, it is highly unlikely that Wright's Prairie houses, built in the first decade of this century, would have looked even remotely as they did if Sullivan's young apprentice had not seen the Japanese exhibit at the much-maligned fair of 1893.

FOUR

As Wright's practice and his family grew, the Oak Park house was expanded several times until it was a rambling complex of buildings, designed both for work and for living. The Wrights had six children, in more or less rapid succession, and Wright found himself, as usual, pressed for money. For this reason he had to accept several commissions for 'traditional' houses that he might well have turned down if his finances had been in better shape. Among these was a large Colonial villa in the neo-Palladian manner, several cottages *à la* Silsbee, and one or two rather severe and classical houses somewhat similar to the Charnley house. But however conventional these houses may appear today, each showed – especially in its interiors – a highly individual style; and the inevitable ornament in friezes and in glass panels was becoming increasingly geometric and very different from Sullivan's curvilinear patterns. Here, in these angular, geometric lines is the first powerful evidence of the influence of Froebel's games upon the formation of Wright's aesthetic preferences.

Wright built his first really extraordinary house in 1893 for a wealthy businessman called William H. Winslow, who had bought a large piece of land in River Forest, a suburb of Chicago close to Oak Park. The Winslow house [3] was an extremely simple, somewhat severe, symmetrical structure two storeys in height, topped off with a pitched roof of terracotta tiles with deep overhangs all around. The ground floor of the house was treated much like the base of any classical building: it was of Roman brick, with simply framed windows of rather horizontal proportions cut into the brickwork. The central, main entrance was set into a panel of decorated tiles, and reached across a flight of low, horizontal steps and a wide terrace. The first floor was expressed quite differently from the ground floor: instead of Roman brick, Wright here used an intricately ornate tile as the finished wall surface, and the horizontal windows were again set into this tile wall. The sweeping roof plane completed the composition.

Anyone looking at the Winslow house today would be struck by the quiet distinction and good taste of its façades, and by the excellence of the workmanship. Less obvious would be those elements that Wright himself has, since 1893, made part and parcel of the vocabulary of American architecture. Yet in 1893 these elements were radical in the extreme; but, unlike much first radical work in the arts, the Winslow house showed such a self-assured handling of proportion and detail that it appears to be the work of an architect who had been doing this sort of thing for many years.

In two respects, particularly, does the Winslow house appear quite masterly: firstly, in the handling of its horizontal composition; and, secondly, in the handling of its scale.

To Wright the horizontal had by this time become the most important architectural line: it was not only that he had been impressed by the dominant horizontal of the traditional Japanese

3. Winslow house, River Forest, Ill., 1893. The first floor is ornamented in the characteristic Sullivan manner. (Photo: Aaron Siskind)

house; rather, he had begun to feel that there was some affinity between nature and architecture – an affinity not as yet quite clearly defined – and that a horizontal architecture tended to suggest harmony with nature, rather than opposition to nature.

Still, here was a two-storey house – not an easy thing to make appear horizontal. Yet this is exactly what Wright set out to do, and succeeded in doing. The first device (starting from the top) was to make his roof a wide, low-slung, low-pitched lid, with a deep brim all around. The roof became a sort of flattened-out tent and dominated the rest of the house completely. Moreover, Wright was able to swallow up some of the height of his second storey within the roof shape, so that the first floor of the Winslow house looks much lower than it really is. Below the roof, there is the device of stratification, of dividing the building into distinctly different horizontal bands. The first floor was a low and long band faced with ornamental tiles; the ground floor was a somewhat higher band made to look long and low because it was faced with Roman bricks, whose shape is long and flattened out. Finally, Wright set his house down, ever so gently, on the lawn, by surrounding it at the base with a continuous step of limestone that projects out beyond the edge of the wall, and by placing a flat terrace in front of the main entrance. Indeed, wherever you look in this house, the horizontal line is the dominant detail: two urns flanking the entrance are horizontal in shape; the double-hung windows are divided horizontally into two long and flat rectangles of glass; and even the entrance door is kept low and squat, rather than tall, simply to accent the dominant line of the composition.

Wright's handling of scale in the Winslow house is just as successful. One of the eternal rules of great architecture is that it must stand up, visually, from two vantage points: from far away, and at close quarters. All great buildings of the past looked well at a distance; their over-all form tended to be simple, somewhat diagrammatic, clearly understandable. At closer quarters, however, the importance of the over-all silhouette would be diminished and the eye would search for new points of interest – smaller-scale detail. The masters of the Acropolis, of the Gothic, and of the Renaissance all knew this truth. Only in recent years has it been forgotten, for much modern architecture looks simple and clear at a distance, but only flat and somewhat dull at close quarters.

In the Winslow house, Wright showed how clearly he understood this principle. For the over-all silhouette of this house is sharply defined, clear, and simple. Only as you approach its front door do the different wall surfaces reveal something new – an intricate play of ornamental detail, a richness of texture quite unexpected from so severe-looking a block. Sullivan, of course, knew the secret of scale-giving ornament and applied it to perfection in his Guaranty building. But even Sullivan never applied it better than Wright did in the Winslow house.

In plan, the Winslow house was as simple and bold as the Charnley house, though there was a much greater play of related, open spaces and of changing floor and ceiling levels. This constant change in the quality of interior spaces was to become an increasingly important aspect of Wright's work; but even more prophetic than the interiors of the Winslow house was a secondary building Wright designed for the Winslow estate – a building to house the stables. Like the main house, the stables were symmetrical in composition (indeed, Wright did not break away completely from classical symmetry until 1908 or 1910). And, like the main house, the Winslow stables were strikingly horizontal in expression, with great sheltering roof tents holding the structure down to the ground. In fact, while the main house was still rather staid and formal, the stables were quite dynamic in appearance and suggested a degree of integration between architecture and landscape which no one had achieved before. (One of Wright's amusing and favourite tricks was employed here: to leave an existing tree undisturbed, he simply left a hole in one of the deep roof overhangs and allowed the tree to continue to grow through it.)

In the sixty-five years after the Winslow house was completed, Wright did much to extend and elaborate upon the basic concept stated there in River Forest, in 1893. But the germ for almost every great idea Wright brought into domestic architecture was contained in that extraordinary house. No architect of the past hundred years was able, in a single work, to produce so complete, so independent a creative statement. When the Winslow house was built, it became clear that Wright was capable of leading American architecture into a new age.

For some years after the completion of the Winslow house, Wright was busy designing large and small homes around Chicago. Some of these were quite traditional (because the client insisted, and Wright needed the money), and there was, in fact, one 'half-timbered' Tudor house of huge proportions which many of Wright's potential clients liked, but which he himself despised. As a matter of fact, the half-timbered theme – a kind of blend of the Japanese post-and-beam frame and the Tudor expression [4] – seems to have left a notable mark on Wright's sense of detail; for it reappeared in some of his most beautiful houses of the early twentieth century. Other designs of the immediate, post-Winslow era were as daring as their precursor at River Forest, though sometimes in rather different ways: for example, Wright began, slowly but quite noticeably, to throw off the strait jacket of symmetry; and though symmetrical elements remained in his houses for many years to come, the over-all composition became increasingly free and dynamic. Finally, some of the post-Winslow houses showed an increasing use of blocky compositions reminiscent of Froebel's geometric games and of overlapping folded roofs that may be traced to Froebelian exercises with folded paper. But in his domestic work Wright did not really advance radically beyond the Winslow house until the turn of the century. When he finally did, the breakthrough was so complete that American architecture is still trying to catch up.

4. Hickox house, Kankakee, Ill., 1900. One of the first, rather 'Japanese', houses, rendered in near-black and white. (Courtesy, Museum of Modern Art)

'The American Nation has a heart and a backbone and a pattern of its own and is rapidly forming a mind of its own,' Wright told an audience at the Chicago Art Institute in the year 1900. What he meant was soon to be revealed in a series of houses whose 'pattern' was a reflection, not only of an entirely new kind of architecture, but of an entirely new way of life.

During the first decade of this century Wright probably built the greatest houses of his lifetime. One of these, the Robie house, [10] completed in 1908, may come to be considered the most influential house of its era. At least half a dozen other houses of the decade are of such extraordinary strength and spirit that each, taken alone, would have assured its architect a prominent place in the history of his art and his time.

The houses of this decade are now known as Wright's Prairie houses, for reasons which are quite apparent: for all have the dominant, earth-hugging horizontal plane, which, in Illinois, means the plane of the prairie. Indeed, these houses have so many things in common that they must be considered elements of a single great work: the creation of a new American domestic architecture.

The horizontality of the Prairie houses was foreshadowed by the dominant lines of the Winslow house. Yet the Winslow house seems monumental and tightly, vertically self-contained by comparison with the sweeping horizontal volumes of the Willits and the Isabel Roberts houses [6 and 7] a dozen years later. For here Wright had at last broken completely with symmetry and substituted for it a dynamic asymmetry, a balance-in-motion infinitely more complex and infinitely more poetic than the formal disciplines of past civilizations.

Horizontality was Wright's response not only to the earth and to the things that grew out of it, but also to the great spaces of America. The Winslow house and, even more so, the Charnley house – these were still, in a sense, 'European' houses; for they reflected the tight discipline required by a densely settled continent. The

5. Coonley house, Riverside, Ill., 1908. A palatial 'Prairie house' with definite 'Japanese' overtones. The projecting roof beams were sheathed in copper. The large planting urns were among Wright's favourite devices in this period. (Photo: Aaron Siskind)

Prairie houses were all space and motion, all dynamism, all America. For this, after all, *is* (or, at least, *was*) the chief characteristic of the New World: space, freedom to move about, an ever-expanding frontier. From Walt Whitman to Jack Kerouac the recurring *American* theme is the open road, the man on the move, the limitless spaces, especially of the Middle West. When Wright built his Prairie houses, he no longer built 'boxes' containing so much usable cubage; he built spaces sheltered under great, sweeping, intersecting, low-slung roof planes – spaces that were open to one another within, and open to the prairie landscape without. Each great horizontal plane would extend from the centre of the house out, beyond the line of windows, into deeply cantilevered overhangs that lead the eye towards some distant horizon, some expanding frontier. These houses were the first dramatization, in three dimensions, of what Whitman meant when he said:

> The earth expanding right hand and left hand . . .
> O highway . . .
> You express me better than I can express myself . . .
> I inhale great draughts of space,
> The east and the west are mine, and the north and
>   the south are mine.

This, the central American theme, was first made architectural in these magnificent horizontal planes-in-motion that Frank Lloyd Wright built around Chicago during that first decade of the century.

Everything somehow evolved out of this central theme: if the road was to be open, then the space within had to be open, and the outside walls had to be open, too. The interiors (except, of course, in areas where privacy was required) consisted of interlocking spaces separated not by doors, but by carefully developed angles of vision. As you moved through those interior spaces, they would unfold in dramatic and ever-changing vistas: everywhere there would be elements of surprise; a sudden, unexpected source of light around a corner, a glimpse of the landscape, a low ceiling after a high ceiling (to be followed again by a high one), a succession of experiences so varied and yet so continuously related that the interior became a symphony of space and light. The boxy, self-contained spaces of the traditional European house were demolished in one fell swoop by a simple, dramatic device: the abolition of closed interior corners. Such corners were simply dissolved in glass, or else resolved by free-standing walls at right angles to one another which never actually met, but, instead, seemed to slide past each other in space. And the theme of space-in-motion was not confined to the insides of the Prairie houses; for each vista from inside out was picked up and continued in terraces and retaining walls that surrounded the house and helped merge the interior, visually, with the surrounding landscape. Every detail of the Prairie house was designed to support this powerful central theme: the roof overhangs were deep and thin-edged; the windows were continuous ribbons of glass, starting directly at the underside of the roof and continuing down to a common horizontal sill line; the parapets of the terraces beyond had continuous horizontal copings of concrete or limestone, and these parapets often would become planting boxes or planting urns which brought elements of nature directly into the architectural composition. As he did in the Winslow house, Wright set his Prairie houses down on the ground with infinite tenderness, stepping down the house around its base until base and lawn were one, or surrounding the house with terraces at gradually descending levels that finally brought the floor line down to natural grade.

In most of the Prairie houses, there would be a central element somewhat taller than the rest – often a two-storey living-room. From this tall central mass, wings would extend in all directions –

6. *Roberts house, River Forest, Ill., 1908. The tall living-room at the centre,
and the low extended wings around it, are typical of Wright's early compositions.* (*Courtesy, Museum of Modern Art*)

first roof planes, then the planes of parapets, finally the low slabs of
terraces – so that the entire house seemed, in the end, to have grown
out of the landscape like some geological formation of horizontal
strata of masonry and glass.

Many of the Prairie houses used the devices of Japanese architecture to achieve their poetic effects. As in the traditional Japanese
house, there was generally a dominant horizontal band inside at
approximately the height of a standard door-opening. This band
continued all the way around the walls and finally emerged on the
exterior as the roof fascia. All added heights were developed above
this low plane, so that many rooms would have intimate, low ceiling
areas (generally around the fireplace) whose height would be just
about that of a standard door, and dramatic, high areas at the centre
where the ceiling would suddenly be formed by the underside of a
pitched roof. In other ways, too, the Japanese tradition came into
play: many of the Prairie houses had a sort of 'turned-up' roof edge
that gave the roof a broken silhouette very similar to that found in
traditional Japanese houses.

In only two respects did the Prairie houses reflect some influence of
half-timbered Tudor: first, in the black-and-white façade with its

darkened posts and beams and its stucco fill-ins, which was somewhat reminiscent both of Japanese and of half-timbered tradition;
and, second, in the matter of small, leaded windowpanes. Wright
very rarely used large sheets of glass in any of his buildings, and in
these early houses his windows were completely broken up into
patterned panes of glass. Much of this mania for leaded glass was
undoubtedly due to Wright's preoccupation with ornament, but
there was another and much more significant reason: Wright
realized that large sheets of glass looked blank, black, and dead
from the outside, and tended to reflect only a single image of nature;
a leaded window or a broken-up expanse of glass tended to look
like a glittering mosaic of many facets and colours when seen from
the outside, for no glazier has ever succeeded in setting two adjoining
sheets of glass exactly parallel to one another. As a result, each little

7. *Plan of Willits house, Highland Park, Ill., 1902. The core of the house is
the hearth, and all wings extend outwards from it. (Courtesy, Taliesin
Fellowship)*

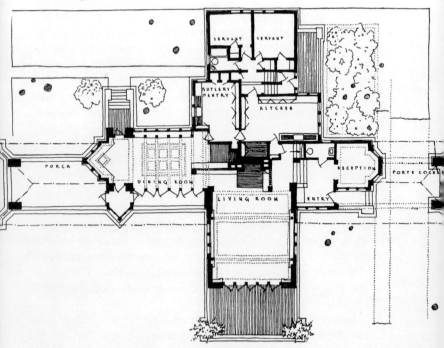

pane of glass reflects a different part of the sky or the sun or the trees, and, instead of appearing dull and dead, a fragmented glass wall becomes a rich mosaic, constantly changing in the light.

'Air, soil, water, fire,' Whitman wrote, 'my qualities interpenetrate with theirs. . . .' In the Prairie houses, Wright established a sort of

8. *Plan of the Martin house, showing the complete merger of architecture and landscape.* (*Courtesy, Taliesin Fellowship*)

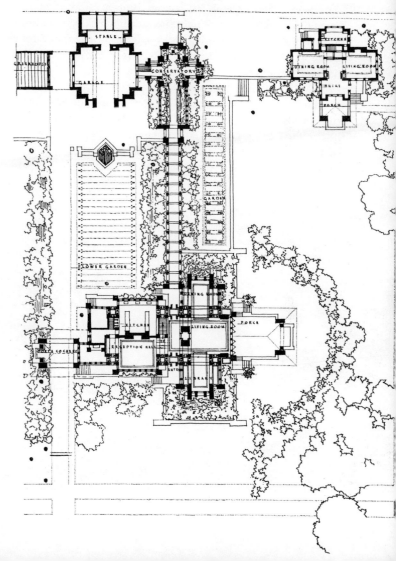

atavistic principle of planning, which remained apparent throughout his work. For at the heart of every Prairie house, there was a fireplace, often of rock, always broad and firmly anchored at the centre of the composition, From this hearth all spaces would extend, radiate into the landscape. This was the source of all life within the house. Beyond that heart, there would be airy spaces, then, quite frequently, pools of water, and, finally, the earth. These primitive elements – water, fire, earth – became a sort of obsession with Wright from the days of the Prairie houses onward. Some thirty years later, when he built his famous Bear Run house over the waterfall in Pennsylvania, Wright succeeded in making the heart of his central fireplace an existing rocky ledge protruding up through the floor; and the third element, water, was, of course, the great theme of that house.

Many of the Prairie houses were not built on the prairie at all, but on suburban sites around Chicago – in River Forest, in Wilmette, in Riverside, and in Oak Park. One of the most beautiful Prairie houses, the one for Darwin D. Martin, was actually built in Buffalo, New York [8 and 9]. Others were built in Rochester, New York, in Wisconsin, and in Ohio. Although their sites were often restricted,

9. Martin house, Buffalo, N.Y., 1904. One of the finest 'Prairie houses', with all the best characteristics of this prototype: low-slung roof planes, ribbon windows, terraces that extend the house into the landscape. (Courtesy, Museum of Modern Art)

10. *Robie house, Chicago, Ill., 1909. This is probably one of Wright's most famous works, and shows all the elements of the 'Prairie' style to perfection: low-slung roof planes, interlocking volumes and masses, sweeping horizontals. (Photo: Hedrich-Blessing)*

Wright succeeded in making the indoor and outdoor spaces seem large by extending interior walls into the landscape, then turning them to form terraces and courts outside the line of the glass.

Fortunately, many of the Prairie houses have survived real-estate 'progress'. The Martin house in Buffalo was destroyed, and the Robie house was almost demolished to make room for temporary dormitories for college personnel. (It was saved by William Zeckendorf, the New York real-estate investor, and restored almost to its original state.) The Coonley house [5] in Riverside, Illinois, a magnificent complex of buildings designed in 1907 and built of stucco and ornamented tiles, looks more beautiful today than ever before. Several of the houses of the period have changed ownership and type of occupancy: one, on the North Shore of Chicago, is now a pleasant restaurant, its double-storey living-room a very effective dining area. But most of them are still in use as residences, and occasionally come on the market to be bought by a growing band of admirers.

It is almost impossible to catalogue the infinite number of innovations in residential architecture which accompanied Wright's development of the Prairie house. Apart from the ribbon window and the corner window, Wright developed a window unit that was a casement opening out, rather than in; he began to plan his houses around a 'utility core'; he dramatized his rooms with 'cathedral ceilings'; he built concrete slab floors directly on the earth without basement, and set the radiant heating systems into that floor. He designed an infinite number and variety of built-in furniture, including storage walls and built-in tables. He employed built-in lighting, including some of the first geometric modern lighting fixtures (which, however, were invariably ornamented with some fairly hideous Art Nouveau frills). He developed the 'car-port' (beginning as the *porte-cochère*). The list could be continued indefinitely, but enough has been said to make it clear that most ideas that characterize the modern American house grew out of the Prairie houses of the first decade of this century.

A good many architects in the history of the art have staked their claim to fame upon much less radical creations than are reflected in the Prairie house. Indeed, very few architects of any time have contributed more than is represented in this work. Yet, incredible though it may seem, the Prairie house was only the beginning, only one facet of Wright's creative genius. For while the Prairie houses were going up, he created an entirely new commercial and industrial architecture as well; and after these two phases of his work had been completed, he began to think in terms of a new kind of structural principle which, in turn, was bound to produce an entirely new kind of architectural expression. So, the Prairie house was only Step One in what was to become perhaps the most prolific creative career his country had ever seen.

SIX

During the first decade of this century, which saw the creation of the Prairie house, Wright was busier than he would again be for a long time. His home in Oak Park was expanded to incorporate a studio; apprentices came to work under Wright's guidance; and more and more clients came to commission non-residential buildings, as well as private houses.

Among the non-residential commissions, there were four or five projects and completed structures of a brilliance and inventiveness as great as any Wright displayed in the creation of the Prairie house. The first of these was merely a sketch: in 1894, or thereabouts, almost thirty years before Mies van der Rohe was to conceive his glass skyscrapers, the American Luxfer Prism Company asked Wright for a design to help promote its new 'directional' glass block. Wright's answer was a project for a slab building, ten storeys in height, whose street façade was to be entirely of glass block and movable glazed sash! This was the first suggestion of a true 'curtain wall' of glass and metal ever made, and the sketch looks as modern today – except for its occasional frills – as any glass-fronted office building put up in any large city in the U.S.A. As the American Luxfer building was designed for a typical site in the middle of the block, it had only one façade – the one fronting on the street. Its side-walls were blank (they were presumed to be party walls), but its rear façade was probably meant to be of glass also. Largely because of the great rectangular simplicity of the design, and because of its blank side-walls, the American Luxfer building is remarkably similar to Corbu's Swiss Pavilion of 1932. Indeed, the façade expression of the structural cage is almost identical with that used by Corbu, and there is a suggestion of some kind of penthouse that breaks the over-all façade pattern not unlike the roof treatment that Corbu used in the Swiss Pavilion. The *pilotis* at the ground-floor level were, however, absent.

Although it is doubtful that Mies or Corbu ever saw the drawings for the American Luxfer project, there is no doubt that Sullivan did see them; and the Schlesinger-Mayer store in Chicago (now Carson, Pirie, Scott), which Sullivan designed and built around 1900, was clearly influenced by Wright's American Luxfer designs. After that, of course, the glass-walled slab building was very much in the air; and it was Frank Lloyd Wright who had put it there.

The second non-residential building of outstanding importance during this period in Wright's life remained a project also: this was a design for the Yahara Boat Club to be built in Madison, Wisconsin, in 1902 [11]. Wright had done several boat-club and country-club structures in earlier years, including a rather massive and ungainly Municipal Boathouse, which was built on Lake Mendota in Madison in 1893. (He had won the job in a competition.) Like the American Luxfer project, the Yahara Boat Club was astonishingly 'modern': it consisted of a simple rectangular block, topped by a long band of glass, and finished off with a deeply cantilevered, flat, slablike roof. The entire composition sat on an extended base of retaining walls that continued far out beyond the limits of the building itself.

This was undoubtedly the simplest, most strikingly geometric design put on paper by Wright up to that time. Quite clearly, its blockiness owed a great deal to Froebel's games; just as clearly, there was evidence of that same horizontal driving force – the driving force of the open road – that dominated Wright's dramatic Prairie houses. But nowhere else until that time had Wright (or anyone else) reduced architecture to so simple and uncompromising a statement.

11. Project for the Yahara Boat Club, Madison, Wis., 1902. One of the most remarkably 'modern' designs among Wright's early work. (Courtesy, Taliesin Fellowship)

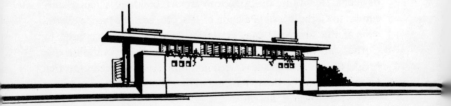

12. Coonley playhouse, Riverside, Ill., 1912. A small, symmetrical, monumental structure, quite similar to the Yahara Boat Club project of ten years earlier. The curious geometric pattern in the stained glass antedates Cubist work in Europe. (Courtesy, Museum of Modern Art)

Perhaps the Boat Club would have shown some of Wright's weakness for finicky ornamentation had it been built. However that may be, the Boat Club stands as a prophetic statement of a great deal of modern architecture which was to be developed by Wright and others in the decades to come: it was prophetic of Mies's Barcelona Pavilion, of much of Willem Dudok's work in Holland after the First World War, and also of Wright's own Usonian houses of the 1930s – especially the beautiful Winkler-Goetsch house of 1939. In this single powerful sketch, modern architecture was given a new and decisive direction.

In the Boat Club – just as in the Prairie houses – the predominant, in fact the *only* movement of space was in the horizontal direction. 'I see this extended horizontal line as the true earth-line of human life, indicative of freedom,' Wright said many years later. The Yahara Boat Club sketch was a really stunning exposition of the extended horizontal line and the extended horizontal space. If one

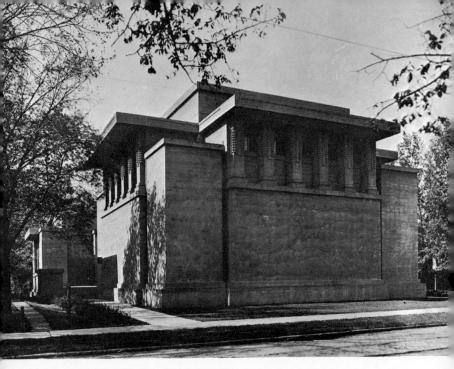

13. Unity Church, Oak Park, Ill., 1906. A monumental, poured-concrete structure of great force. (Courtesy, Museum of Modern Art)

thinks of 'space' as a sort of invisible but ever-present vapour that fills the entire architectural volume, then Wright's notion of space-in-motion becomes more clearly understandable: the contained space is allowed to move about, from room to room, from indoors to outdoors, rather than remain stagnant, boxed up in a series of interior cubicles. This movement of space is the true art of modern architecture, for the movement must be rigidly controlled so that the space cannot 'leak' out in all directions indiscriminately. The controlling element in the Boat Club was the sweeping horizontal roof plane and the long side-walls; both directed the movement of space horizontally outward, in a single plane. A few years later, as Wright's mastery of the art of manipulating space became more profound, he began to play with space moving in all directions. In the Yahara Boat Club, the manipulation of space was much less complex and thus, perhaps, all the more dramatic.

Unity Church, which resembles the Boat Club in many respects, was actually built in 1906, in Oak Park [13]. It is one of the most important buildings in Wright's career, and one of the best. Basically, the building consists of two separate blocks: an auditorium, more or less square in plan, and a parish house, which is rectangular and linked to the auditorium by the narrow 'neck' of an entrance loggia. The entire building was of poured concrete – Wright's first use of this material – and its composition was even more blocklike than that of the Boat Club. However, Unity Church was not nearly as horizontal in emphasis as the Boat Club: both of its elements were at least two storeys in height, with different levels and balconies projecting out from the walls into the tall central spaces. Like the Boat Club, Unity Church had a solid base, topped by a band of windows which, in turn, were held down by the projecting lid of a flat roof-slab. Like the Boat Club, Unity Church was also very simple and modern in composition, and all small-scale texture and ornament was restrained and noticeable only at very close quarters: there was a little ornamentation on the window mullions, and some textural pattern in the concrete, achieved through the use of a coarse, pebbly aggregate.

These are, however, relatively superficial characteristics of the building. Its true importance lies in three specific aspects: the organization of its plan and all that this implied; the organization of

14. Plan of Unity Church. The two principal wings are separately articulated, and joined by an entrance-link. This plan-diagram has since become a standard in modern architecture. (Courtesy, Taliesin Fellowship)

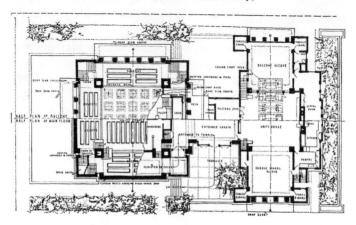

49

its spaces; and the quality of its linear, geometric, interior ornament.

The plan of Unity Church looks familiar to us today simply because it is the prototype of thousands of eminently successful types of modern plan, from houses to city halls [14]. Here, for the first time, we find an absolutely clear-cut demonstration of the articulated, 'binuclear plan', or 'H plan' – the plan that every functionalist, from Le Corbusier to Marcel Breuer's young American students, has found an eminently satisfactory solution to the organization of a multifunctional building. What the H plan does, in effect, is to separate the two principal, opposing functions of any given building – in a house, the daytime living areas versus the bedrooms; in a city hall, the administrative block versus the council chamber – and link these opposing functions with a narrow 'neck' that also serves as the principal entrance to both elements of the building. This arrangement works beautifully because the entrance link, being at the centre, makes each part of the plan equally and independently accessible.

Some critics have claimed that the functionalists' preoccupation with separating functionally different elements from one another grew out of Cubist tradition – or, specifically, out of the tradition of Russian Constructivism after the First World War. Possibly so; but the evidence of Unity Church, built in 1906 and widely publicized throughout the world, suggests an earlier source for the principle of separate articulation – one of the really fundamental principles of modern architecture.

The second important aspect of Unity Church is the manner in which Wright handled the space within. In the Boat Club this space was conceived of as a horizontally moving entity; here, at Unity Church, the volumes are tall and complex in their height. Balconies intrude into the auditorium and the parish house at various levels. And, more importantly, light intrudes from the sides *as well as from above*, for the roof is no longer a solid horizontal lid, but a giant 'egg crate' of skylights, so that the space within is drawn upward, sideways, and, indeed, in all directions.

Here, for the first time, Wright developed an entirely plastic space. (The Larkin building, in Buffalo, which was built in 1904, showed

51

some of these possibilities, but did not come as close to realizing them as does Unity Church.) Before long, Wright would be completely fascinated by the possibilities of truly plastic, multi-directional movements of space, and would come to the recognition of an entirely new concept of structure through this understanding.

Unity Church is where I thought I had it [Wright recalled in later years]; this idea that the reality of a building no longer consisted in the walls and roof. So that the sense of freedom began which has come into the architecture of today and which we call organic architecture.

Finally, there was the linear geometric ornament used throughout the auditorium in particular. This linear ornament consisted of long bands of flat trim, occasionally forming squares and rectangles in dynamic and asymmetric compositions. Each of these linear patterns was closely related to the architectural element to which it was applied: the balconies, the pulpit, the lighting fixtures, the skylights. What it all added up to was simply this: in the interiors of Unity Church [15], Wright – almost casually, almost as an afterthought – laid the foundation for one of the most important movements in modern design, the movement formed in Holland a dozen years later and known as 'De Stijl'. Wherever one looks in the auditorium, one can see Mondrian's paintings in the flesh – a dozen years before Mondrian! There can be no question whatever that the Dutch De Stijl painters and architects had seen the exhibition of Wright's work in Holland in 1910 and that they were familiar with his Unity Church. Thus we find Wright giving birth, almost absent-mindedly, to one of the most influential and one of the most powerful groups in the entire history of modern art.

The curious and amusing aspect of all this is to be found in the twists and turns that aesthetic influence will take: Wright's geometric ornament in Unity Church was intimately, 'organically', related to the structure, to the different volumes within the space, and to the manner in which these volumes might help him manipulate the space within. Then the De Stijl movement came along and took the *surface* patterns of Unity Church, ripped them off the architecture that had produced them to begin with, and began to play with the patterns for pattern's sake, to make them a discipline of graphic design. Indeed, van Doesburg, in particular, later used the geometric pattern to *destroy* certain architectural spaces, rather than help underline the architecture! Finally, the young International

16. *Larkin Co. administration building, Buffalo, N.Y., 1904. A monumental block owing little to anything except, perhaps, the spirit of American industry as expressed by silos and similar structures. (Courtesy, Museum of Modern Art)*

Style men in Europe, finding Mondrian and van Doesburg more 'modern-looking' than Wright, with his slightly Victorian fussiness, took over De Stijl, reinterpreted it as a three-dimensional discipline (relating it again to structure, mass, volume, space), and presented the whole thing to the world as a new sort of architecture! In one sense, of course, it was; for Wright was rarely able to get away completely from the stigma of nineteenth-century taste, and the International Style did succeed in doing that. But when Wright said, in 1928, that 'all Le Corbusier says or means was at home here in architecture in America in the work of Louis Sullivan and myself, more than twenty-five years ago, and is fully on record . . .' he may, perhaps, be forgiven for his arrogance: for Unity Church, in its plan, in its spatial organization, and in its linear ornament, was indeed one of the most fertile sources for all of twentieth-century architecture.

Two years before Unity Church was completed, Wright built several important structures in Buffalo, New York, for Darwin D. Martin, whose own beautiful Prairie house in that city has been mentioned earlier. Through Martin, Wright got the job of designing the Larkin Company administration building, the first entirely air-conditioned modern office building on record [16]. In some ways the Larkin building resembles the Boat Club and Unity Church: like them, it is blocklike and extremely simple in its forms, and has very little ornamentation. But here the similarity ends; for the Larkin building was as decisively vertical as the Boat Club was horizontal. Indeed, it was the first consciously architectural expression of the kind of American structure which Europeans were beginning to discover to their delight: the great clusters of grain silos and similar industrial monuments that men like Corbu and Gropius found so exciting in the early 1920s. Indeed, the Larkin building was, in a sense, a squared-off silo – monumentally simple and powerful. But it was a great deal more than that, for the space within – the 'reality' of the building, as Lao-tze put it centuries ago – was very different from the space within a silo.

It was a very dramatic and simple space: in the centre, a four-storey well, topped by a huge skylight; and around this well, galleries of office space open to the centre shaft of light and air. Here the movement of space was entirely vertical, and every detail helped accent that fact. But the walls of the Larkin building were not tight enclosures by any means.

I think I first *consciously* began to try to beat the box in the Larkin building [Wright said years later]. I found a natural opening to the liberation I sought when [after a great struggle] I finally pushed the staircase towers out from the corners of the main building, made them into free-standing, individual features.

Suddenly, the enclosure – the need for enclosure – melted away, and it was possible to develop the space within the building in all directions without fear of hitting a blank wall.

For this building, Wright designed lights, desks, office chairs, and other fixtures and furnishings of metal and glass [17] – extraordinary, spidery, Constructivist-looking objects (fifteen years before the

17. *Interior of the Larkin building. Like most of Wright's urban structures, this one was lit primarily from above, thus shutting out the surrounding townscape. All fixtures and furnishings in the building were designed by Wright. (Courtesy, Museum of Modern Art)*

Constructivists came along) – objects that seem occasionally odd and complicated in retrospect, but, when squinted at, suddenly appear remarkably similar to today's articulated furniture designs produced by the spearheads of our current avant-gardes. As for the office planning techniques employed, these must have seemed radical in the extreme in their day: all-steel files, for example, were built flush into walls and into partitions in modular combinations; and all secretarial spaces were treated as open, flexible 'pools' that could be subdivided at will if need be.

Every book on modern architecture published in Europe in the 1920s carried pictures of the Larkin building. It was probably the most widely admired American structure (apart from the Robie house) of the first decades of this century. Yet the City of Buffalo, in 1949, sold the building for a few thousand dollars to a wrecking firm, for salvage. It seems that nobody at Buffalo City Hall knew very much about that old pile of bricks in their midst, and so it was sacrificed to progress.

By 1909 Wright was, in all probability, one of the best-known architects in America. Nowadays, this fact is not very widely understood, for there has grown up a myth about Wright to the effect that his great native genius was ignored by his own countrymen and only recognized by Europeans for what it really was. This is nonsense; between 1889, when Wright built the first section of his house in Oak Park, and 1909, twenty years later, when his two most beautiful Prairie houses – the ones for Avery Coonley and Frederick C. Robie, respectively – were completed, Wright had actually built something like 140 houses and other structures! In addition, he had completed nearly fifty projects for various clients, and many of these were widely published and exhibited. Indeed, Wright's work took up an increasing share of the annual exhibitions at the Chicago Architectural Club from 1894 onwards; so much so, that an entire room was set aside for his work alone in the Club's annual show in 1902, and a special and major section of the show's catalogue was devoted to Wright's work. There was, as a matter of fact, a good deal of grumbling over the growing prominence given to Wright by the Club's 'Hanging Committee', and, because of this, Wright withdrew from the Club's annual exhibitions for a period of time. Nevertheless, either he and his work sought the limelight, or the limelight sought him: his houses were published everywhere (the *Ladies' Home Journal* actually commissioned him to design one of the first Prairie houses for its readers); and he was asked more and more often to speak before professional and lay audiences.

One of the most significant lectures Wright gave during that period, the Hull House Lecture, was entitled *The Art and Craft of the Machine*. Wright first delivered this lecture in 1901, then revised it several times for later delivery before various other audiences. The Chicago Architectural Club, in 1901, reproduced the lecture in full in its catalogue (instead of showing any of Wright's work that year), and its influence was therefore widespread and probably strong.

Here, almost twenty years before the Bauhaus, Wright stated certain principles of art in an industrial civilization – and, specifically, in an industrial democracy – which are as valid today as when they were first formulated.

The machine is here to stay [Wright announced]. There is no more important work before the architect now than to use this normal tool of civilization to the best advantage – instead of prostituting it as he has hitherto done in reproducing with murderous ubiquity forms born of other times and other conditions. . . . [Words always tended to roll off Wright's tongue in great melodic torrents. He was a true disciple of Whitman, in every way!] Genius must dominate the work of the contrivance it has created.

In other words, unlike the latter-day functionalists, Wright never believed that the machine look was an essential result of machine fabrication. 'This plain duty [of dominating the machine] is relentlessly marked out for the artist in this, the Machine Age.'

This was perhaps Wright's most important pronouncement at Hull House, but it was by no means his *only* important statement of principle. Although most of the functionalists against whom he would wage war in later years were still in their short trousers, Wright seems to have had a premonition of some of the theories that were bound to spring up sooner or later – theories he would have to fight as vigorously as Sullivan fought the systems of the neo-classicists. 'I believe that only when one individual forms the concept of the various projects and also determines the character of every detail in the sum total . . . will unity be secured which is the soul of the individual work of art,' Wright said at Hull House. This is, of course, in diametric opposition to the theories later to be propounded by Gropius and others, who believed that architecture in the modern world (a world of 3,000,000,000 human beings) must be the product of teamwork. It is true that Gropius felt that the architect was the only 'specialist' equipped to be a universal man, and that he should therefore head the team and coordinate its work. But, even so, teamwork was the key slogan of Gropius's kind of society; whereas 'unity through individual creativeness' became, as early as 1901, the key slogan in Wright's theory of a democratic architecture.

In all likelihood, Gropius and Wright were not nearly as far apart as it may have seemed at various times in their lives. But to Wright the issue had to be drawn with the utmost precision, without compromise. *Genius and the Mobocracy* was the title he gave to his later biography of Sullivan. The true danger in a time of mass populations was, in Wright's mind, that democracy would become ruled by the mob; whereas the American ideal, to him, implied the dominance of the free individual – free to act creatively and to live creatively within a minimum of necessary limitation. In later years, when Wright became identified increasingly with 'liberal' politics (he was so 'liberal', in fact, that the Communists were able to dupe him on occasion to lend his name to causes they wanted to see promoted), other 'liberals' found it very difficult to understand why, for example, he opposed Roosevelt's New Deal with such passion. The reason was simple. Roosevelt, in Wright's mind, had done two things that were alien to the American democratic ideal: he had centralized and strengthened governmental power (instead of decentralizing and weakening it in the direction of the anarchist ideal); and he had handed this power to 'the mob' (rather than depend upon individual genius to act creatively and on a large scale). That much of this was nonsense (for Wright's theories of how to run *anything*, from a school to a nation, were somewhat dubious) did not detract from the purity of Wright's nineteenth-century principle; indeed, he was considerably more liberal than most of his latter-day 'liberal' admirers.

The version of the Hull House Lecture delivered to a gathering of the Daughters of the American Revolution, in 1904, contained some passages on the American city which form a permanent and beautiful contribution to the literature of the United States.

Thousands of acres of cellular tissue, the city's flesh outspreads, layer upon layer, enmeshed by an intricate network of veins and arteries radiating into the gloom, and in them, with muffled, persistent roar, circulating as the blood circulates in your veins, is the almost ceaseless beat of the activity to whose necessities it all conforms. . . . If the pulse of this great activity . . . is thrilling, what of this prolific silent obedience? Remain to contemplate this wonder until the twinkling lights perish in groups, followed one by one, leaving others to smother in the gloom; until the fires are banked, the tumult slowly dies to an echo here and there. Then the darkened pall is lifted and moonlight outlines the sullen, shadowy masses of structure deeply cut here and there by half-luminous channels; huge patches of shadow, shade, and darkness intermingle mysteriously in block-like plan and skyline; the broad surface of the lake beside, placid and resplendent with a silver gleam. And there reflect that the texture of the tissue of this great machine, this forerunner of the democracy we hope for, has been deposited, particle by particle, in blind obedience to law – the organic law to which the great solar universe is but an obedient machine, and marvel that this masterful force is as yet untouched by art or artist. . . .

From the day of his arrival in Chicago, when young Frank stood outside Wells Street Station in a drizzle, with 'sputtering white arc-lights in the station and in the streets, dazzling and ugly . . . crowds. Impersonal. Intent on seeing nothing' – from that day on, Wright both hated and loved the city: hated it for its money-grabbing ugliness; loved it for its brute vigour. In all his life he was never able to cope with the city successfully. Unlike Corbu, he could never approach it rationally. Where his country buildings seemed, literally, to melt into their environment, his city buildings were invariably a kick in the teeth of their surroundings. Yet all through his life he wanted to try to find a way to make the city mesh.

During these successful years of Wright's professional life, his family grew up close to his Oak Park studio: the two oldest children, Lloyd and John, were destined to become architects; next there was a girl, Catherine; after her, another boy, David, now an executive with a firm manufacturing concrete blocks; then another girl, Frances and another son, Llewelyn. Mrs Wright, in effect, operated a sort of kindergarten; Wright insisted that each child should learn to play a musical instrument (a heritage of William Wright's pre-occupation with music). He himself would often sit down at the piano to play Beethoven's music. 'His eyes closed, his head and hands swaying over the throttles, I think he imagined he was Beethoven,' John Lloyd Wright recalled many years later. 'He looked like Beethoven. . . .' As a matter of fact, Wright was extremely handsome in a romantic sort of way, and knew it. (The only picture of him taken during those years was one *he* took by means of squeezing a long rubber tube while sitting in front of his own camera!) Wright was very much of a ladies' man, and he was attracted to some of his clients' wives as much as the wives were to him. He liked to dance, and to go out riding on horseback and, later, in a roadster that he himself had redesigned.

I think this car had something to do with Papa's leaving home [John Lloyd Wright has written]. I know it added new values to his life, for it was at that time that an attractive young woman fell in love with him, or he with her, or both with each other. They went riding often.

The attractive young woman was the wife of a neighbour, Edwin Cheney, for whom Wright had built a small house in 1904.

> Everything, personal or otherwise, bore heavily down upon me [Wright said later]. Domesticity most of all. What I wanted I did not know. I loved my children. I loved my home.

Yet he no longer loved Catherine, and marriage without love seemed to him a crime. He asked for a divorce, but Catherine refused. Finally, he took the decisive step: in the autumn of 1909 he abandoned his family as his father had abandoned his. With Mrs Cheney, Wright took off for New York and Europe, leaving his practice behind in something close to chaos. Their first stop was Berlin, where the publisher Ernst Wasmuth was preparing the great publication of Wright's work up to that time. After spending some time with Wasmuth on this volume, Wright and Mrs Cheney went on to Florence, where they rented a little villa to escape the newspaper publicity their flight from Chicago had caused. 'I now sought shelter there in the companionship with her who, by force of rebellion as by way of love, was then implicated with me,' Wright wrote in his *Autobiography*. They stayed until 1911, and then returned to the United States. By that time the Wasmuth edition of Wright's work had been published in Berlin, and a parallel exhibition of his work had been shown throughout Europe. Overnight he had become the most widely discussed architect of the day. Every young European architect tried to find out all he could about Wright's work and principles. Only in America, where the scandal press had used Wright's private life as a means of attacking his work, did he seem to be losing ground.

EIGHT

Unhappily, the publicity resulting from Wright's affair with Mrs Cheney was only the beginning of a whole series of private disasters that were soon to be turned into public scandals. For the moment, however, Wright's life seemed to be settling down to something close to normality. Upon his return from Europe, he decided that he wanted to build a new home for Mrs Cheney and himself.

I suppose that faith carried . . . me through the vortex of reaction, the anguish and waste of breaking up home and the loss of prestige and my work at Oak Park [Wright recalled]. Work, life and love I transferred to the beloved ancestral Valley where my mother . . . had bought the low hill on which Taliesin now stands and she offered it to me now as a refuge. . . . I began to build Taliesin to get my back against the wall and fight for what I saw I had to fight for.

Taliesin is the name of a mythical (or at least legendary) Welsh poet. The word actually means 'shining brow', and it was around this shining brow at Spring Green, Wisconsin, that Wright began to build a new home for Mrs Cheney and himself.

Taliesin East (as it was to be called later) has undergone many transformations – some of them, as we shall see, violent in the extreme. Today it is a vast, rambling complex of buildings with many courts – several houses, in fact, rather loosely joined together. The original Taliesin East was rather small – a Prairie house in the best tradition, joined to a studio wing that, in turn, was linked to stables, a barn, and a garage. It had all the beauty of the typical Prairie house and most of its characteristic detail: low-slung pitched roofs with deep overhangs; and ribbon windows that created an intimate relationship between the interior spaces, the surrounding gardens, and the rolling Wisconsin landscape beyond. The scale was established by the low eave-height inside and out, which, in turn, was dramatically contrasted with the high roof ceilings in less intimate spaces. Most of the furniture was built in; all of it was of the blocklike, geometric variety Wright had come to like and to build especially for his houses whenever possible. The décor throughout was Oriental – Japanese prints, figures of Buddha, valuable Chinese vases, etc. But Taliesin East showed the influence of the Orient in a more profound way as well: the classical, European approach to a building is direct, straight, monumental; the Parthenon is approached that way, and every European building of the classical tradition has been approached in this straightforward manner. But the typical Japanese house or temple is approached quite differently: there may be a gate, and then a hedge or fence that forces one to turn, and then a walk through gardens, up a few steps and down a few steps, more turns through smaller and larger gardens past pools, and so forth – until suddenly a corner of the building is visible behind some planting. And only after the final turn does the visitor see the building revealed, more or less in full. Taliesin East was designed in exactly that way – not on paper, not diagrammatically, but by a great artist capable of visualizing a progression of spaces and forms, a changing of vistas, a play of surprises, and of light and shade from unexpected sources. (Medieval European architecture has some of these same characteristics, and this is the only European tradition Wright ever admired.)

Wright had made his first trip to Japan in 1905 and had become completely enchanted with the traditional architecture of the islands. He had actually donned Japanese dress and travelled through many of the smaller towns and islands to see, in their native setting, what he had first come across in the small Japanese Pavilion at the 1893 exhibition. Despite his furious denials, it was quite obvious that the Japanese house had long influenced his own work to a high degree; and his love for Japanese prints – the only decorative art (excepting his own ornament) he ever tolerated in his buildings – dates from that trip. So Taliesin East became an American house in the Japanese tradition.

Still, it was a very radical reinterpretation of that tradition. For one thing, Taliesin East, like the Hillside Home School that Wright had built in Spring Green for his two maiden aunts, Nell and Jane Lloyd-Jones, in 1902, was constructed largely of local stone, in massive piers that seemed to grow right out of the earth. For another, the plan of Taliesin East, though entirely open in the living areas, was compartmented for privacy in the sleeping areas. Finally, the floor of Taliesin East was virtually on a level with the surrounding land to facilitate the 'marriage' of indoor and outdoor space, whereas the traditional Japanese house, for practical reasons of flood and earthquake resistance, is elevated on short stilts.

Yet the principles of planning were very similar, and there was no particular reason for Wright to deny this, except that he insisted upon denying all influence upon his work other than Sullivan's. The latter's influence upon Wright did, indeed, crop up about this time in a remarkable project Wright prepared for the *San Francisco Call*: the twenty-four-storey press building to be built on Market Street in the downtown area of the city. Two versions of the press building were designed by Wright; the more interesting of the two was a free-standing tower, a thin and wide monumental slab of Sullivanesque proportions. Here was Sullivan's base, shaft, and cap rendered with tremendous verve. This was to be a soaring skyscraper, with strong vertical piers growing straight out of the sidewalk and continuing all the way up to the top floor. A sweeping roof overhang, much deeper than the one at the Wainwright building, topped off the skyscraper. Like the American Luxfer building, this project, though unbuilt, was remarkable in its modernity. Except for the treatment of its cap, the building resembled many of the finest slab structures by Mies and others developed in later years.

Shortly after the press building project was completed. Wright was given one of the largest and most spectacular commissions of his career: the design of the Midway Gardens restaurant in Chicago [18]. In many respects this group of buildings represents a new point of departure in Wright's work, in the direction of greater ornamenta-tion and greater complexity. The programme for the Midway Gardens suggested some of this: it was to be a combination casino, resort-restaurant, and place for outdoor concerts.

What Wright produced here was, in effect, a huge complex of terraces and turrets, of masses and volumes on intersecting levels so playfully manipulated that a new kind of spatial experience seemed to be suggested by them. These intersecting levels raised the horizontal into the third dimension, suggesting a movement of space upwards and downwards, as well as parallel to the plane of the earth. In a sense the Midway Gardens are an urban architectural elaboration of the terraced gardens at Taliesin East; indeed, Midway Gardens, as its name suggests, was largely outdoors, a spacious central court surrounded by ascending terraces and buildings.

Perhaps the most remarkable fact about Midway Gardens was

18. *Midway Gardens, Chicago, Ill., 1914. A fantastically ornamented structure that shows the first influences of Mayan architecture upon Wright.
(Courtesy, Museum of Modern Art)*

the nature of its ornament – both that designed by Wright (generally
of patterned concrete block) and that by the sculptor Ianelli, whose
figures were placed on pedestals and parapets all around the central
court. This ornament, done in 1914 quite independently of any
Cubist developments in Europe, was almost entirely abstract in
character. Just as Wright had, in a sense, invented the De Stijl
movement at Unity Church, so he anticipated much of the later
Cubist work in painting and sculpture at Midway Gardens. Again,
this significant innovation was merely incidental to the architecture;

it was certainly a necessary part of the volumes and spaces – an organic part in that each abstract turret or figure helped underline the movement of space and the ascent of the brick masses – but it was not at the heart of the architectural problem, which, as usual, was one of manipulating space. In short, Wright had once again, almost casually, given the other arts a helping hand. Unfortunately, this masterpiece was soon to be torn down: for various reasons the enterprise was never very successful, and Prohibition gave it a final blow from which it could not recover. The Gardens were replaced by what Wright called an 'auto-laundry'.

'When the Midway Gardens were nearly finished,' Wright recalled in his *Autobiography*, 'my son John and I . . . were sitting quietly [one day] eating our lunch in the newly finished bar.' Suddenly there was a long-distance telephone call from Taliesin East. There had been a terrible tragedy: a Barbados Negro, a servant at the house, had suddenly gone berserk, killed seven of the inhabitants of the house, and set fire to the buildings. Mrs Cheney and her two children were dead, and so were four apprentices and workmen. The living quarters were demolished; only the working areas survived. It was a tragedy of such monumental proportions that Wright was completely numbed. He buried Mrs Cheney himself,

and no monument yet marks the spot where she was buried [he wrote later]. All I had left to show for the struggle for freedom . . . had now been swept away. Why mark the spot where desolation ended and began? . . . The gaping black hole left by the fire in the beautiful hillside was empty, a charred and ugly scar upon my own life.

For days Wright himself seemed hardly to be alive. He slept, or tried to sleep, in the studio wing that had been untouched by fire. Armed men searched the hills for the madman, who was finally caught. The numbness that had overtaken Wright probably spared him some of the horror of the newspaper publicity that grew out of the tragedy – for, of course, the scandal sheets loved the whole affair. Here was this mad architect, this freethinker, this radical who had run off with a married woman and left his own family in the lurch; the man had obviously received his just deserts. And wasn't this sort of scandal just what you would expect from people who lived in crazy-looking houses? The yellow journalists tried to destroy Wright, not only as a man, but as an architect as well. 'As one consequence of the ugly publicity . . . hundreds of letters had come to me from all over the country,' Wright recalled. 'I tied them up together in a bundle now and burned them. Unread. I went to work. The salt and savour of life had not been lost.' And Wright performed a supreme act of courage: he went on living.

NINE

Some time after the Taliesin tragedy, Wright received a very sensitive and understanding note of sympathy from a complete stranger – a sculptress called Miriam Noel – and he answered it gratefully. Shortly thereafter, Miss Noel turned up in Chicago. She was a striking woman of great sophistication and elegance, quite unlike anyone Wright had ever known before. In his loneliness he felt drawn to her, and they became intimate friends.

Meanwhile Wright had obtained one of the best-known commissions of his career – the job of building the new Imperial Hotel in Tokyo to replace an earlier Imperial Hotel that had burned down during an earthquake. The manager of the hotel and a commission of advisers had made a trip through Europe and the United States to find an architect to do the job, and when they saw Wright's houses around Chicago, they were instinctively drawn to him. By 1915 Wright and Miriam Noel were in Japan, and Wright, especially, loved every moment of it. He felt that here was a civilization complete in every detail: from prints to clothes, from music and poetry to architecture, there was not a single false note. 'How can anything human be so polished and clean?' Wright asked. And, for the first time, he was willing to admit that

if Japanese prints were to be deducted from my education, I don't know what direction the whole might have taken. *The gospel of elimination of the insignificant preached by the print came home to me in architecture. . . .*

Thirty years later, when Wright attacked Mies's credo of 'less is more', he seemed to have forgotten some of those earlier words.

Yet his stay in Japan was not pure bliss by any means. There were serious financial and political difficulties in connexion with the planning of the Imperial Hotel; but, more disturbingly, there were difficulties connected with Miriam Noel. It turned out that she had had a fairly long history of mental instability, and there were serious emotional crises of the most morbid kind. Wright blamed himself;

he was still unable to marry her, because Catherine would not agree to a divorce, and his self-recriminations hardly added to his own happiness.

The planning of the Imperial Hotel took many months. It was to be an extremely complex building – complex not only in its plan, but also in its structure. In plan Wright tried to do something similar to what he had achieved at Midway Gardens – an infinite variety of spatial experiences, surprises, and delights, all scaled to the small size of all things Japanese. In structure he tried to solve the terrible traditional problem of Japan – how to combat earthquake tremors.

This problem was complicated by the fact that the site on which the Imperial Hotel was to be built consisted, as Wright put it, of 'eight feet of cheese-like soil that overlay ... liquid mud'. There seemed to be no way of getting any kind of solid support for the building, so Wright determined to 'float' its foundations on this bed of mud, rather than try to find some solid support deeper down. The next problem was how to keep the building from cracking up like hard icing on a base of jelly once the jelly begins to shake. Wright decided that there was only one way, and that was to make the building itself of many small and independent parts to start with, rather than wait for the next earthquake to do it for him in an unpredictable way. Thus the Imperial Hotel was made of many sections with 'expansion joints' between them – sections that could move independently of each other if the need ever arose.

Still, such sections were often as much as sixty feet in length. A fair-sized earth tremor could easily crack this, so Wright developed a system of structural supports that were a stroke of pure genius. 'Why not carry the floors as a waiter carries his tray on an upraised arm and fingers at the centre – balancing the load?' Wright asked. Why not indeed? It was something the Japanese had *tried* to do in their wooden houses supported on individual posts (the idea being that if one or two posts were lifted up or lowered by the earth tremors, the wood frame of the house could absorb the strain and would eventually return to its original shape as the tremors subsided). But in the traditional Japanese house the posts were around the perimeter of the building, so that an earth tremor *anywhere* under the house would be bound to affect its structure. A wooden structure might be able to resist such strains, but the monolithic concrete-and-steel buildings going up around Tokyo were bound to crack under the impact.

So Wright put his concrete 'posts' or 'fingers' under the centre of each section of the Imperial Hotel, and then cantilevered the floor slabs out from that pin-supported centre in all directions, letting the slabs touch the perimeter walls only very lightly. These walls, in turn, were supported on systems of pins or fingers as well, so that each part of the building was allowed, in effect, to move independently and then to return to its original position.

Wright's clients thought he was utterly mad, but his persuasiveness carried the day for him again and again. On one occasion, when the building was almost completed, a severe earthquake shook the structure – and left it completely undamaged. After that, Wright was given his way in almost every respect. However, one of the conditions imposed upon him was that he would stay in Tokyo until the building was finished. So, he and Miriam Noel remained in Japan until 1921, with only a few trips to Taliesin in between. Wright was thus able to control every detail, every decorative touch, every single item of cabinet work put into the Imperial Hotel. The result was an unparalleled bit of fantasy – delightful, charming, and slightly unbelievable [19].

To begin with, on its surface the Imperial Hotel was one of the least 'Japanese' buildings Wright had done up to that time. Why this was so is hard to explain: perhaps he was trying to prove to someone (possibly himself) that he had not been influenced by Japanese tradition at all. In any event, the Imperial Hotel is one of his first faintly Mayan temples – an astonishingly ornate and rich structure strongly reminiscent of the temples at Chichen Itza in Yucatan [20]. It is as if Wright had tried, subconsciously, to return the compliment by bringing something beautiful of the western hemisphere to the Japanese islands.

But in its scale, and in its play with surprise elements, the Imperial Hotel is completely Japanese. Wright was apparently so struck by the smallness of Japanese things that he made everything in the Imperial Hotel tiny: in some of the rooms the glazed doors leading out to little balconies are hardly more than five feet high; elsewhere, windows overlooking gardens and courts are so low that one must get down on all fours to enjoy the view. (On the other hand, the doorknobs on guest-room doors are so high that the small Japanese maids must stand on tiptoe to reach them – possibly an intended effect, as Wright liked the grace of Japanese women.) There were little terraces and little courts, infinitely narrow passages suddenly

19. *Imperial Hotel, Tokyo, 1916–22. A rich blend of Mayan ornament, Japanese scale and detail – all drawn together by Wright's picturesque genius. (Courtesy, Museum of Modern Art)*

20. *Banquet Hall in the Imperial Hotel. The ornament is largely derived from American-Indian themes. (Courtesy, Museum of Modern Art)*

opening out into large two- or three-storey spaces; big and little pools (both for ornament and to provide water for fire-fighting during earthquakes, when the municipal water system tended to collapse). And there were many different levels, both inside the rooms and outside the buildings, including connecting bridges between the two long, parallel wings of guest-rooms. Finally, Wright achieved something almost unheard of in hotel design: in this most standardized of all fields of cubicle architecture he succeeded in making almost every guest-room different from every other. In short, he created a hotel that would be an efficiency expert's nightmare, and a pure delight for any guest.

Two years after he left Japan, a terrible earthquake struck Tokyo and destroyed much of the city. One hundred thousand people perished. There was utter confusion in the press reports reaching the United States; for several days the papers said that the Imperial Hotel was completely destroyed. Wright could not believe it. Finally, there arrived the famous telegram that is now part of architectural history:

> HOTEL STANDS UNDAMAGED AS MONUMENT OF YOUR GENIUS HUNDREDS OF HOMELESS PROVIDED FOR BY PERFECTLY MAINTAINED SERVICE CONGRATULATIONS

It was signed by Baron Okyra, Wright's great friend, the Chairman of the Board of the Imperial Hotel. The virtually untrained, untutored country hick from the Middle West had shown himself to be one of the finest engineers of his time.

In spite of this and other professional triumphs, Wright's life remained complicated and unhappy. Miriam Noel's condition had gone from bad to worse; finally, Wright was able to persuade Catherine to grant him a divorce so that he could marry Miriam. He hoped that this would help her emotional balance, but, if anything, her health deteriorated after their marriage. Suddenly she left Taliesin – where the Wrights had gone after their return from Japan – to live in Los Angeles. After consultation with a psychiatrist, it became obvious to Wright that their marriage, too, was beyond repair. They were divorced in 1927; she died in a sanatorium a few years later.

TEN

On the surface, Wright's work was becoming more and more ornate; in plan and spatial organization, it was becoming increasingly
complex. Compared to the Yahara Boat Club of twenty years
earlier – that unbelievably modern, clean-cut composition of sweeping, flat planes – the Imperial Hotel looked old-fashioned and
fussy. What exactly was happening to Wright? Was he simply
growing old?

What was happening had been suggested here and there by details
found in his work for a couple of decades: he was beginning to
discover a new kind of space entirely, and with it a new kind of
structure. To all great architects, the 'reality' of a building is the
space within and around it, not in its plan and elevations. Wright
was always fond of quoting (or paraphrasing) Lao-tze and pointing
out that 'the reality of the vessel is the void within it'. To Wright
the walls, roofs, floors, frills, and all the rest were merely tools of
the trade – the raw materials with which an architect must work.
But the potential greatness of architecture was the quality of the
space within and without.

In his early buildings – the American buildings that paralleled
Whitman's 'open road' – Wright had felt that his kind of space
should be a horizontally moving entity, always controlled in layers
parallel to the earth. Such spatial movement tended to produce an
architecture of soaring flat slabs, all directing the eye towards some
distant expanding frontier, some far-off prairie horizon. But somewhere along the line – at the time of the Larkin building and of
Unity Church – Wright began to sense the possibilities of space-in-
motion up and down as well as sideways. He began to sense the
excitement inherent in changing levels, in light appearing not only
through horizontal bands of glass but also through huge skylights
above, of progressions through architecture involving not only turns
and twists, right and left, but ascents and descents as well.

Something of all this had been in the back of his mind from the days when he first saw Sullivan's ornament for the interiors of the Auditorium.

The magic word *plastic* was used by the Master in reference to his ornament, and the room itself began to show the effects of this ideal [Wright wrote in his *Autobiography*]. The ideal began to enter the Auditorium interior. Not consciously, I believe. Subconsciously . . . while no advantage was taken of the arched elliptical form [of the theatre] to carry the loads above . . . still the form was appropriate, suitable to its purpose and prophetic.

Just how prophetic it was Wright himself did not realize until several years later. But Sullivan's ornament had two tremendously significant characteristics, which eventually led Wright to a new architectural concept: the ornament was 'plastic' and it suggested 'continuity'. The most characteristic form in Sullivan's ornament was a spiral form, generally made up of bent and twisted grasses or twigs, with no beginning and no end. This form in nature is, of course, the snail – a structural organism of extraordinary sophistication completely unmatched by man, at least until Wright began to try to match it.

His first attempts in that direction were relatively crude: the low ceiling planes of the roof-overhang carried into the house, contrasting with high ceilings formed by the pitched roof itself; the steps up and down within open spaces; and the occasional hidden slot of glass somewhere inside the folded roof structure which permitted streaks of sunlight to move, like long fingers, across walls and floors as the earth rotated. This sort of thing had been done before, though rarely with such subtlety and art. But now Wright tried to create a new kind of structure to enclose and enfold the continuous spaces that, he felt, were suggested by structures in nature – structures like sea-shells, cobwebs, and cocoons.

From Unity Church onwards, Wright had sensed the enormous potentials of concrete reinforced with strands of steel.

Concrete is a plastic material [he wrote]. I saw a kind of weaving coming out of it. Why not weave a kind of building? Then I saw the shell. Shells with steel inlaid in them . . . Lightness and strength! Steel the spider spinning a web within the cheap, plastic material.

To describe the special characteristics of reinforced concrete, Wright liked to fold his hands tightly and then try to pull them apart. 'The steel strands are there to resist tension,' he would say, 'and the concrete resists compression. Together, the two can resist any stresses from any source.' The plasticity of concrete, he went on, inevitably opened up an entirely new world of form. Not only did it make the right angle and the box obsolete, it actually made them inefficient. The great thing was to let the stresses in floor, walls, and roof flow into one another without any dividing line at any of the traditional corners – to allow the plastic concrete to work just as in a sea-shell, making it both the structure and the enclosing skin.

How radical this concept was can be understood only when one looks at the 'skin and bones' architecture of Mies and of most classical architecture of the past. Wright liked to demonstrate the (to

21. 'Hollyhock House' for Miss Barnsdall, Los Angeles, Calif., 1920. A fantastic 'Mayan Temple', rendered in exposed poured concrete. (Photo: Ezra Stoller)

him) old-fashioned character of post-and-beam structures by holding up the index finger of his left hand and placing his other index finger on top of it horizontally, to form a T. 'You see, this is the old post and beam principle,' Wright would say, wiggling the two fingers to show the inherent instability of such a structure. 'It is only as strong as its connexion. But in a continuous structure of concrete,' he would go on, now folding his hands and trying to pull them apart, 'the strength is in the organic form itself.'

So, the natural forms of Sullivan's Art Nouveau ornament led Wright to a re-examination of the structural (rather than ornamental) qualities of forms in nature. And he came up with a principle – continuity – which, for the first time in the history of architecture, represented an effort to conquer the problems of structure by the use of forms found in nature for millions of years. To the list of his masters – a list bearing only Sullivan's name until then – Wright added that of Nature herself.

One of the tragedies of Wright's life is that technology never quite caught up with him in his own lifetime. Indeed, not until the last few years of his life did engineers and other architects begin to grasp the possibilities of shell structures in which there were no longer skin and bones, but only a thin reinforced skin so warped and twisted as to give it tremendous structural strength. One engineer – Professor Mario Salvadori at Columbia – used to demonstrate the principle to his students by picking up a thin and flat sheet of paper, holding it at one end, and making it flap up and down. 'You see, the skin has no structural strength at all now,' he would explain. Then he would pick up the same sheet of paper at one corner, give it a warped shape by twisting it between his fingertips, and try again to make it flap around. But now the sheet had become quite rigid and was capable of supporting itself without trouble. Wright grasped this principle from the early 1920s on, but he did not have the technological tools to demonstrate it properly until many years later. As a matter of fact, at the time of his death in 1959, certain plastics engineers were just beginning to experiment with reinforced and irradiated plastics that promised the kind of structure Wright had prophesied during the latter part of his life.

Wright's first conscious attempts to create such continuous plastic structures were made in the year after he returned from

23. *Living-room in Ennis house, Los Angeles, Calif., 1924. One of several concrete-block houses of the period, using a specially designed, ornamented block, and a mesh of reinforcing rods to tie the masonry together. (Photo: Ezra Stoller)*

Japan. One of these was a house he designed for Mrs Alice Millard, in Pasadena, California. Here he tried to use concrete – a specially and ornately patterned concrete block – and a mesh of steel reinforcing rods to create a strong fabric for all floors, walls, and roofs, strong in tension as well as compression. This sense of an interwoven structure was expressed on the outside by a gridlike ornament – again very Mayan in character, and very geometric. Within, the spaces were on several interlocking levels, with fingers of sunlight penetrating the space from many secret and surprising sources. In the following year, 1923, Wright built two more of these 'woven fabric' houses, both in Los Angeles – one for Dr Storer, and the other for Charles Ennis [23]. Here again the ornament and exterior composition were Mayan; and while the Millard house was still rectangular in its silhouette, the Ennis house had several walls and masses that tapered upward, creating an effect of greater plasticity in form than was apparent in the rectangularity of the Millard and Storer houses.

Wright's preoccupation with reinforced-concrete block continued throughout his lifetime, and three of his sons were involved in these experiments in one way or another. Lloyd and John Lloyd Wright, both architects, were helping him directly on the early California houses. David became an executive with a company manufacturing concrete blocks, and continued his interest in his father's experiments throughout the latter's life. Actually, the idea of reinforcing modular concrete blocks with steel rods, vertically and horizontally, and then pouring concrete into the hollows of the blocks to 'weld' the steel to the concrete makes considerable sense and is used frequently in more run-of-the-mill construction. But by its very rectangular nature the concrete block did not really lend itself to the

24. First Unitarian Church, Madison, Wis., 1950. A folded-roof structure designed on a diamond-shaped module. The peak is meant to represent hands raised in prayer. (Photo: Ezra Stoller)

sort of plastic expression Wright was trying hard to achieve: a building of concrete blocks was almost bound to be rectangular in its overall shape. (Many years later, when Wright built his extraordinary concrete-block house for his son David, he probably 'bent' and 'twisted' the block as much as it can possibly be bent and twisted. But this was strictly a *tour de force*, and not a serious attempt to find a widely applicable solution.)

By the same token, Wright was severely handicapped in his attempts to introduce plasticity into wood-framed houses. The straight wooden stud or joist is a very hard thing to bend, and Wright never quite succeeded in bending it. What he did do was try to fold it. Some of his designs of the early 1920s – particularly the cabins he designed for a projected summer colony on Lake Tahoe – look very much like the folded paper games that were part of his Froebelian upbringing. While a folded plane is not as inherently strong, structurally, as a moulded sheet, it does possess a structural strength much greater than that of any post-and-beam-and-skin building. Still, it was only the beginning, and Wright was quite obviously frustrated by the terrible limitations imposed upon him by the straightness of available building materials.

Yet the twin notions of continuity and plasticity obsessed him for the remainder of his life. He saw that here was a principle so new, so tremendously important to the future of architecture that all those who seemed to stand in its way were on a par with the Beaux Arts academicians who had barred the way to Sullivan in 1893. What the International Style men were building in Europe was, to Wright's way of thinking, another kind of box – stripped of neo-classical ornament, but still a box with straight posts and beams, straight sides that ended up being just another sort of strait jacket. There was no chance for a free, democratic architecture, Wright felt, until man could make buildings unbend, until the building could be shaped by the desired flow of space in any and all directions. Such buildings would be truly 'organic', for not only did they express the aspirations of free men to free space, but they also expressed a kind of structure that had within it all the elements of living things in nature – muscles, tendons, fibres, skin – all woven together into a single organism acting in unison. 'Nature is right, but man is straight,' Thoreau had written. 'She erects no beams, she slants no rafters, and yet she builds stronger and truer than he.' To Wright, American architecture had to be Nature's architecture – organic,

25. *Auditorium of Madison Unitarian Church. The diamond-shaped space creates an intimate enclosure, lit from various unexpected sources. (Photo: Ezra Stoller)*

flexible, free. Conversely, he felt, all straight, post-and-beam architecture was, in effect, an expression of a straight-laced, autocratic, European concept of society.

Much of this sort of argument was, of course, rather far-fetched. The Japanese post-and-beam house, in which the walls were literally dissolved into the garden landscape beyond, had seemed to express a concept of freedom to Wright only a few years earlier. And in his later Usonian houses Wright himself frequently returned to rectangular geometry closely related to the post-and-beam concepts of the traditional Japanese house. Yet the obsession with fluidity and plasticity of structure remained; if he was not always able to express it in his houses, in particular, the reason lay in the straightness of available American building materials. Indeed, most of Wright's truly 'plastic' designs prior to 1945 remained projects on paper. Only in a few of the last great buildings of his career did he finally and completely break through the grid of rectangular geometry to demonstrate what he meant by an 'organic' architecture.

In later years, as part of his attempt to break through 'the box', Wright discovered that a hexagonal, diamond-shaped, or triangular module might work almost as well as a square one, and produce an infinitely greater variety of spaces. This fascination with polygonal shapes may be traceable to Wright's experience with Silsbee's informal cottages, whose inevitable bay windows were, generally, half a hexagon or half an octagon. Indeed, Wright's first experiment with non-rectangular forms came not long after he left Silsbee: this was a sixty-foot-high windmill and water tower built at Spring Green for his two aunts – a structure that, for somewhat far-fetched reasons, Wright insisted upon calling Romeo and Juliet ever after. The structure, in plan, consisted of a diamond-shaped spine being 'embraced' by a somewhat shorter, polygonal tower – hence (apparently) 'Romeo and Juliet'. In any event, this very charming structure contained within it not only a suggestion of future modular patterns in Wright's work, but also a prophecy of folded-skin structures not very different from the Lake Tahoe cabins of several decades later.

When Wright returned from Japan and built his handful of California houses, he was well past fifty. His fame was completely assured. His work was published everywhere; and though most of the publicity surrounding his unhappy personal life was not conducive to making him widely accepted or respected by conventional society, his name was revered among imaginative young architects everywhere. He had built or projected hundreds of structures, each more inventive than the ones preceding it.

Meanwhile, in Europe, Le Corbusier and Mies van der Rohe were just beginning to make names for themselves. Neither had built more than a couple of houses, or designed more than half a dozen 'ideal' projects. Wright, in short, had a tremendous head-start over those who would soon begin to challenge him. On the other hand, in the eyes of the new European modernists he remained somewhat tainted with the excessive frills and finicky tastes of the nineteenth century. He was never quite able to overcome this handicap, never quite able to become 'more modern' than he had been in the Yahara Boat Club project and in Unity Church. But despite his tendency towards fussiness in detail and ornament, he held firm to his great central convictions about the nature of space and of structure; and in these areas he remained ahead even of younger generations until the end of his life.

ELEVEN

The 1920s were years of recurring disaster and unhappiness for Wright. Shortly after his separation from his second wife, Taliesin East once again caught fire, and the living areas were once again destroyed.

> During the terrible destruction [Wright wrote] the crowd stood there on the hill-top, faces lit up by the flames. . . . Some were already sneering at the fool who imagined Taliesin could come back after all that had happened there before.

Yet Wright went back to work, rebuilding his home once more.

Then his mother died at the age of eighty-three. She had been very close to him throughout his life, and had come to visit him in Japan during the building of the Imperial Hotel. And Louis Sullivan died, destroyed in part by public indifference and neglect, in part by alcoholism. Wright and Sullivan had met again and resolved their quarrel before his death, and Sullivan gave his disciple the first copy of his own autobiography, with a dedication. The copy was destroyed in the fire at Taliesin in 1924.

And whatever happened, and wherever it did, the press was there to cover the event. Wright was hounded by Miriam Noel and her lawyers, and he was hounded by creditors. There were fewer and fewer clients. Except for a couple of old and faithful friends, like Darwin D. Martin, or a relative like Richard Lloyd-Jones, almost no one came to Wright. It was not that he was insufficiently well known (indeed, he hired a newspaperman to keep his name *out* of the papers, but the effort was a failure); it was simply that there was an air of instability about him and his life, and few potential clients were willing to risk their money with him.

And things continued to get worse: Wright was still in debt over the rebuilding of the first Taliesin when the second version burned down. To build Taliesin III, he went into debt more deeply than ever; everything he owned was mortgaged to the hilt. Moreover, there had been a further complication: in the early days of his separation from Miriam Noel, Wright had met Olga Lazovich, the daughter of an aristocratic Montenegran family, and they had fallen in love. Olgivanna, as he called her, had been married before and had a daughter by that first marriage. Her former husband teamed up with Miriam Noel's lawyers and before long Wright – now married to Olgivanna – found himself a fugitive from justice, being arrested under all sorts of warrants sworn out by either Miriam Noel's lawyers or those of Olgivanna's former husband. Moreover, he was unable to meet his obligations under the mortgages on Taliesin III, and the banks foreclosed. Wright found that the only way to save Taliesin was to incorporate himself and to sell shares on his potential earning power to his wealthy friends. This he did, and the Taliesin Fellowship was founded.

During these nightmare years Wright managed to build or project a few things of lasting value. How he did it is almost incomprehensible in retrospect; he was constantly in and out of the headlines, in and out of the courts. In all likelihood, it was the quiet strength of Olgivanna which saw him through. One of his finest works of these

26. Taliesin, Spring Green, Wis., 1925–59. Many levels, many courts, and many unexpected vistas make this one of the most subtle spatial compositions of our time. (Photo: Ezra Stoller)

years was Taliesin III [26], rebuilt from 1925 onwards, and still partly under construction when Wright died thirty-four years later. At Taliesin III Wright created one of the most beautiful rooms of his career – a living-room of many spaces, all flowing together under the great central roof ceiling. Here were most of the finest elements that Wright had brought into domestic architecture: the heart of the house, a great rocky fireplace with a huge boulder for a lintel; a skylight so placed as to allow a streak of sunlight to animate this rugged chimney breast [27]; a symphony of roof levels, some low and intimate over sitting areas, others high and spacious over places where people might gather at a party; a play of many different materials and textures – stone from the Wisconsin hills, natural wood, plaster in a natural sand colour; built-in furniture of every sort, with the characteristic horizontal blockiness that had become Wright's personal idiom; and planting everywhere, indoors and out. There is hardly a more romantic room than this in America.

The 1920s were, of course, the great skyscraper-building years in America; and though Wright did not get a chance to build one until after the Second World War, the seeds for his various skyscraper concepts were sown in this difficult period.

Wright had two major difficulties of a philosophical sort in design-ing a skyscraper: first, as a believer in an architecture close to nature, he had a hard time justifying a tall, upright, seemingly anti-nature building; and, second, his obsession with the twin concepts of continuity and plasticity – a preoccupation that had led him to the sea-shell and the cocoon as ideal structural prototypes – made it difficult to approach the design of a tall, multicellular building (there are no really tall sea-shells). He solved this dilemma in a character-istic fashion, by going to the one source in nature which did suggest a way of building a tall structure: the form of a tree.

In structural terms a tree is a vertical beam cantilevered out of the ground. Most of its mass is above the ground, and most of the stresses applied to a tree – such as wind pressures and snow loads – are applied to it high up, close to its crown. The structural force that keeps a tree from toppling over is, of course, the restraint applied to its roots by the earth in which they are embedded; and whenever a storm blows up, the wind pressures are counteracted by pressures applied by the earth.

This sort of cantilever is, as a matter of fact, one of the simplest and most dramatic expressions of continuity, for it represents a

27. *Guest-room at Taliesin. The streak of sunlight moves across the chimney breast in the course of the day and makes the space come to life. (Photo: Ezra Stoller)*

delicate balance of forces, each restraining the other through an infinite number of strands and fibres which make the tree a continuous organism. To Wright, the cantilever was also the 'most romantic, most free, of all principles of construction', and so he again applied a natural principle he had grasped by intuition, and demonstrated its eminently practical aspects in terms of engineering. Instead of designing a cage of columns and beams as Sullivan had done (with the outer row of columns practically in a plane with the outer walls), Wright designed a skyscraper prototype whose central, vertical core was the only structural support! This was a kind of tree trunk, deeply anchored in the soil; and floor slabs were then arranged to spread out like horizontal branches from this central trunk, so that the outside skin of the building had to carry no loads at all and could be made of glass, metal, plastic, or any other light and thin material [28 and 29]. The central trunk was to be of reinforced concrete, and would contain all services as well – elevators, ducts, wiring, and piping.

Wright first explored this principle in a project for the National Life Insurance skyscraper in 1924. Here, however, the core was not a single trunk, but rather a series of trunks spaced apart on a regular module. The chief difference of this system from Sullivan's typical cagelike structure was that there were no columns in the exterior walls. The walls were to be simply of glass set in copper strips.

By 1929, however, Wright had really designed his concrete-and-glass tree just the way he wanted it: the vertical service core was the trunk, and all utilities were contained within this vertical shaft. All floors were cantilevered out from it, and the exterior skin was simply sheathed in glass and metal. This project – the famous apartment tower for the vestry of St Mark's-in-the-Bouwerie in New York – was never built, but Wright returned to the basic concept again and again; finally, in 1954, in Bartlesville, Oklahoma, Wright was able to build his St Mark's tower – twenty-five years after it was first designed.

While Wright was developing his concrete-and-glass trees in America, Mies was designing his own glass skyscraper on an exactly parallel principle in Germany. Indeed, the 1920 skyscraper by Mies was considerably further advanced in concept than Wright's first sketches of the same year for the National Life Insurance building, and not until the St Mark's tower, nine years later, did Wright come close to Mies's bold concept.

Whether or not Wright was influenced by Mies's widely publicized sketch and model is difficult to know; needless to say, Wright would have denied such influences, and Mies would, in all likelihood, prove too modest to make any such claims. Yet the two projects are so similar that it is very tempting to compare them and to discover what, exactly, makes them so very different in ultimate expression.

It should be said from the start that Mies's glass skyscraper was a brilliant but rather abstract sketch, whereas Wright's tower was a very detailed proposal, full of practical suggestions for such things as movable metal partitions, built-in cabinets, mechanical equipment, and so on. By necessity, therefore, Mies's sketch seems bold and simple, whereas Wright's appears slightly over-complicated. Granting all this, however, Mies's glass shaft was sleek, slender, vertical, and utterly modern, whereas Wright's tower was full of fussy ornamental touches and conflicts between vertical and horizontal articulation. (He obviously still preferred the horizontal, but knew from Sullivan that a horizontally accented skyscraper will

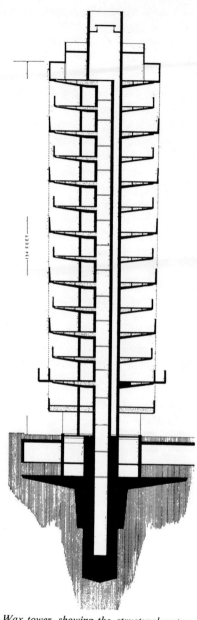

28. Section through the Johnson Wax tower, showing the structural system employed. (Courtesy, Taliesin Fellowship)

always tend to look like a candy stick.) Both Mies's and Wright's towers were irregular in plan outline, but Mies's was completely free-form in a very modern and, incidentally, a very 'plastic' way, whereas Wright's tower was based upon a diamond-shaped module, and its silhouette therefore looked rather jagged, almost in the manner of the Italian Futurists of the pre-First World War era. Yet the principle that motivated Mies's and Wright's designs was identical; the only difference was that Mies happened to be a generation younger and very much 'in the swim' of the new ideas in the plastic arts then current in Europe; whereas Wright was something of a cultural isolationist, with an eye only for what was happening in the Far East – rather like the political isolationists in America between the two wars.

The increasing jaggedness of Wright's forms and details was the direct result of his use of triangular or polygonal modules. One reason why he used these modules was that they seemed to him to relate to geometric formations found in nature. 'Crystals,' he said, 'are proof of nature's matchless architectural principle.' What he tried to build was a crystallic architecture – at least in the cities.

Imagine a city iridescent by day, luminous by night, imperishable! Buildings, shimmering fabrics, woven of rich glass; glass all clear or part opaque and part clear, patterned in colour . . . to harmonize with the metal tracery that is to hold all together. . . . I dream of such a city.

It was a lovely picture. But when these words were spoken, Corbu and Gropius were trying to solve the problem of the huge urban centre in very different terms. Their approach was based upon certain social convictions that were far removed from Wright's thinking, and it was based, also, upon a concept of civic art which remained unintelligible to Wright throughout his lifetime. What he was really trying to do was to make the city look more like a natural organism.

The gleam of mineral colours and flashing facets of crystals. Gems to be bought and set; to forever play with light to man's delight, in never-ending beams of purest green, or red or blue or yellow, and all that lives between. Light! Light in the mathematics of form. . . .

He was describing the romance of jewels, but he might as well have been describing the romance of the sort of crystal city he liked to dream of in his studio at Taliesin.

Did this crystal city make as much sense as Corbu's Ville Radieuse? Probably not. But it did have something Corbu's city did not have – at least not in the northern, 'Gothic' sense of Wright's Wisconsin.

Why should architecture or objects of art in the machine age . . . have to resemble machinery [Wright asked]? Modern architecture . . . will become a poor, flat-faced thing of steel bones, box-outlines, gas-pipe and hand-rail fittings, as sun-receptive as a concrete sidewalk or a glass tank. [This was twenty years before Mies built the Farnsworth house.] Without romance the essential joy of living as distinguished from pleasure is not alive. The new romance is that reality.

Wright may have been a cultural isolationist, but he knew exactly what he was isolating himself from.

TWELVE

Wright's founding of the Taliesin Fellowship in the late 1920s was not merely a way of escaping his creditors by selling shares in his own practice. It was also the start of one of the most extraordinary schools of architecture in the modern world. For many years young people from various countries had approached Wright and asked to be allowed to serve an apprenticeship in his studio. This sort of thing has always been standard procedure in the training of young architects, and Wright accepted these apprentices in ever-growing numbers. Finally, in 1929, with the founding of the Taliesin Fellowship, the arrangement was made more formal: young men and women could come and work at Taliesin under Wright's direction for a fee, and many did.

The Taliesin Fellowship has often been criticized on two grounds: first, because (it is alleged) the young people who came to study there were, in effect, exploited and forced to do all sorts of housekeeping and farm work, rather than learn something about architecture. And, second, the Fellowship has been criticized because it did not produce any very talented 'Wrightian' architects.

To some extent both criticisms are justified. The young men and women who came to Taliesin were required to do everything from peeling potatoes to sweeping the floors. But to Wright this did not seem to be a form of exploitation at all. For one thing, he despised formal education and felt that all it could teach was formulas – not principles. (His own education had, of course, been of the most informal sort.) It seemed to him that there were only two or three things one could teach: firstly, a basic understanding of nature, and he could think of no better way of teaching that than to make his apprentices work on a farm as he had done in his own youth. Secondly, he believed that it was important to convey the need for utter dedication to work, for architecture is no dilettante affair. And, finally, Wright believed that all you could really teach was a *principle*, and even that could only be hinted at in talks, in music,

93

and in working on things that seemed to express that principle.

It is fair to say that through the years the Taliesin Fellowship has produced no great architects. One of the problems was that Wright tended to be resentful and sometimes even jealous of any young upstarts who dared to question ideas or actual projects under development at Taliesin. In this respect he was, however, no more intolerant than Mies, who felt, while he was director of the School of Architecture at I.I.T., that no young student had the equipment to challenge fundamental ideas until he had absorbed some of the principles of architecture through hard preparatory work. But Wright's Taliesin, being inextricably tied to a great individualist, produced only 'yes men'; whereas Mies's I.I.T., under the leadership of one who had made a fetish of anonymity, gave an occasional chance to those who held ideas very different from Mies's own. Thus the only Taliesin apprentices who have shown any great promise in their independent careers are found among those few whom Wright expelled from the Fellowship for what he considered to be their youthful arrogance!

Wright's thoughts on education were somewhat unusual, as they began with the assumption that the basis of architectural education was to reject just about every precedent. In 1930, when the Fellowship was just getting under way, he said that 'any architect should be radical by nature because it is never good enough for him to begin where others have left off'. At the same time, he never cared much for 'radicals' in his own Fellowship, and any young man who dared challenge Wright's ideas was in danger of expulsion. His own justification of this apparent contradiction was that there *were* a few precedents that should be adhered to under all circumstances. 'The workings of principle in the direction of integral order is your only safe precedent, now or ever,' he told his young apprentices. 'The circumference of architecture is changing with astonishing rapidity, but its centre remains unchanged, the human heart.' Still, the apprentices insisted upon copying the details and the mannerisms in Wright's work without apparently understanding the basic principles of spatial and structural organization beneath the often fussy detail. Indeed, it is fair to say that Wright's influence was considerably greater upon those who never went to Taliesin, for some of these younger architects saw through the Art Nouveau trappings a great and shining ideal, and explored it further in a more modern idiom. Shortly after the end of the Second World War, a group of apprentices got together to create a community of Usonian houses near Pleasantville, New York. The result was depressing: except for one singularly beautiful house by Wright himself, located (of course) on the highest point of the development, there were only near-caricatures of the master's own earlier houses – sadly distorted, lacking in scale, utterly unrelated. A French lady visitor whose English was not fluent, and who was taken to Pleasantville by a U.S. State Department guide to get a glimpse of what the American avant-garde was up to, returned somewhat baffled by the whole experience, stating to a friend that she had been to a community called, she thought, Insomnia Homes. It was an unwittingly accurate commentary, not only upon this settlement, but upon much of the work produced by former members of the Fellowship.

Slowly, very slowly, Wright's fortunes began to improve after his own personal disasters and after the Wall Street crash, which had hurt him as much as it hurt every other architect. In the early 1930s his work was again being exhibited, first at the Chicago Art Institute (whose Wright exhibition was widely circulated); and next at the Museum of Modern Art in New York, where, in 1932, Wright was one of the architects included in the now famous International Exhibition of Modern Architecture. The work of Corbu, Mies, Gropius, and others of the 'younger' generation was shown next to Wright's, much to his chagrin. He had by this time begun to consider himself in a special class entirely, and he had made no secret of this or of his contempt for the architects of the International Style – although he had earlier expressed his admiration for Corbu, Mies, and Gropius on many occasions. 'I believe Le Corbusier [is] . . . extremely valuable, especially as an enemy,' he had said. And later, in speaking of Corbu's delight in proportional systems: 'Le Corbusier, hard as nails and sane as a hammer up to this point, goes as superstitious as a milkmaid lost in the mist of a moonlit night' when speaking of systems such as the Golden Section. Moreover, Wright had made it perfectly clear to Henry-Russell Hitchcock, one of the organizers of the Museum of Modern Art exhibition, what he considered his own position in architecture to be: 'I warn Henry-Russell Hitchcock right here and now that, having a good start, not only do I fully intend to be the greatest architect who has yet lived, but the greatest who will ever live. Yes, I intend to be the greatest architect of all time.' That, it would seem, just about settled that.

Yet, despite his anger at having his work exhibited next to that of

Corbu, Mies, and others, Wright benefited considerably from the experience. For he was forced, much against his will, to *look* at what the younger men had been up to in Europe; and this look did him quite a bit of good. For the next six or eight years much of Wright's work suddenly became as 'modern' as any done by Mies or Corbu: the Art Nouveau ornament disappeared; flat, undecorated surfaces and sweeping planes took the place of the filigree of the Imperial Hotel and the concrete-block houses in California; and there were even some buildings with large uninterrupted panes of glass. For a relatively brief moment Wright became almost an International Style architect himself! Then one day he appears to have heard a comment to this effect, and he angrily turned his back upon the International Style for ever. Still, during the few years after the Museum of Modern Art exhibition, Wright produced some of the greatest buildings of his long and fruitful career.

THIRTEEN

During the 1930s Wright built four structures of a beauty unexcelled in America before or since. The first of these, in 1936, was the famous Kaufmann house at Bear Run, Pennsylvania – the house that was cantilevered out over a waterfall. The second, completed in 1938, was the administration building for the manufacturers of Johnson Wax, in Racine, Wisconsin. The third, a group of buildings begun in 1938, was Taliesin West, Wright's winter headquarters in Paradise Valley near Phoenix, Arizona. And the fourth was really a structural prototype: the so-called Usonian house, a dwelling Wright developed in the late 1930s and executed, in several variations, during those years. Wright was now in his sixties; and, while his fortunes were gradually improving, he was denied any part in the three most important building projects of the decade: the construction of Rockefeller Center in New York, the building of the Chicago Fair of 1933, and that of the New York World's Fair of 1939. Yet, in retrospect, it was Wright's work in those years that did most to advance American architecture.

The Kaufmann house, built for the head of a Pittsburgh department store, is probably the most poetic statement Wright ever made – and the most complete statement of his romantic beliefs [30]. Here all the ancient, atavistic elements have been invoked to create a temple dedicated to nature: the rocky ledge on which the house rests; the massive boulder that is allowed to penetrate the floor of the living area to form the hearth; the fire at the centre of the house; the waterfall below; and the great sweeping cantilevers, almost incredible in their daring, that extend from this core of rock, fire, and water and thus carry the eye to the landscape beyond.

The Kaufmann house is remarkably simple by Wright's standards: a geometric composition of horizontal concrete planes (the cantilevered balconies) played against vertical stone planes (the walls and fireplace). It is so simple, indeed, that the influence of the International Style can hardly be denied. Yet it has no boxiness whatever:

30. Kaufmann house, Bear Run, Pa., 1936. This dramatic structure is cantilevered out over a natural waterfall. The core of the house is a rocky ledge, which forms the hearth of the fireplace. (Photo: Hedrich-Blessing)

all interior corners are dissolved in glass, all interior spaces extended across broad balconies into the landscape. In short, the spatial continuity is assured by much the same means Wright had perfected since the days of the Prairie houses. And the structural plasticity – which, to Wright, must inevitably go hand in hand with spatial continuity – is more dramatically expressed than ever before in the great reinforced-concrete cantilevers balanced on the small rocky ledge above the waterfall.

While the Kaufmann house was nearing completion, Wright began work on another structure, which demonstrated even more clearly what he meant by continuity and plasticity. This was the Johnson Wax building, a horizontal version of Wright's Larkin building of thirty years earlier [31]. Here again there was a great space – a secretarial pool – lit almost entirely from above, with

31. *S. C. Johnson & Son Inc. administration building, Racine, Wis., 1936–9. All structures are curvilinear since their plan is based on a circular module. Window-ribbons and the roof of the main office space are of glass tubing. The supporting columns are of concrete, shaped like huge golf-tees. The laboratory tower was completed in 1930. (Photo: Ezra Stoller)*

mezzanines cutting into the central space at various levels and containing more important individual offices. Yet where the Larkin building was Wright's architectural version of the vertical grain silo, the Johnson Wax building was a flattened-out structure of great horizontal bands of brick alternating with glass tubing; and where the Larkin building was all squared-off and blocklike, the Johnson Wax building was softly rounded, its module being the circle.

Here, as at Bear Run, Wright produced a structure of startling modernity, as sleek and undecorated as anything built by the International Style. But while this seems particularly striking today in view of his earlier and later fondness for ornament, the sleekness of the Johnson Wax building is only a surface manifestation. Its true importance lies again in what Wright achieved here in terms of structure and in terms of space.

The basic structural unit designed by Wright was a very slender, tapered, tall concrete mushroom, a little like a giant golf tee [32]. This elegant column was delicately balanced on a small brass shoe embedded in concrete at the main-floor level. There were more than eighty of these concrete tees, and each carried either a mezzanine floor level, or the roof, which, like the bands of glass in the exterior walls, consisted entirely of glass tubing welded together. As a result, the great central room, a space of about 230 square feet, looks like a lovely grotto lit mysteriously from above, and inhabited by a forest of graceful stalactites. Here again the cantilever principle is employed in all its grace, for each of the concrete tees is, in effect, a balanced structure whose great circular crown is cantilevered out from the tapered shaft. No one believed that this structure would stand up, for there were then no rule-of-thumb methods of calculating any structure other than a post-and-beam cage. To get even a conditional building permit, Wright had to erect a test column on the site and load it with sandbags to the point of ultimate failure. The Racine city engineers were as baffled as everyone else (except Wright) when the test column proved to be capable of carrying many times the loads it would ever be required to bear.

Structural plasticity and spatial continuity here again went hand in hand. The space enclosure looked very thin-shelled – as, indeed, it was – because by alternating bands of brick with bands of glass tubing, Wright made clear in the exteriors that this wall was merely a screen and carried no loads. Meanwhile, the bands of glass tubing gave the interiors a recurring rhythm of light, much of it from unexpected angles. Even at the intersection of roof plane and exterior wall, where 'box architecture' would inevitably have a cornice or a sharp dividing beam, Wright destroyed the corner by creating a soft and rounded transition of glass tubing. In fact, the building has no corners at all; every space flows into every other, gracefully, naturally, without a moment of hestitation. It is one of the finest demonstrations of space-in-continuous-motion which Wright or anyone else has ever achieved.

33. *Taliesin West, Phoenix, Ariz., 1938–59. The great wooden girders at the left span the studio and support its canvas roof. The masonry is 'desert concrete', i.e. a mixture of huge rocks and cement poured into wooden forms.* (*Photo: Ezra Stoller*)

To enumerate in detail or even catalogue the innovations to be found in this one building [Wright announced airily] would require more time and patient attention on your part, and mine too, than either of us care to give it. So let's say here that it is technically, and in the entire realm of the scientific art of Architecture, one of the world's remarkably successful structures. I like it. They like it. Let it go at that.

Just for once, Wright was not exaggerating one bit. The building, moreover, attracted so much attention – and, hence, free publicity – that the advertising man for the Johnson Wax people estimated that his company received more than $2,000,000 worth of free advertising at the opening of the structure alone! And the company has been using the building in its advertising ever since.

Taliesin West [33–8] was begun by Wright in 1938, and, like Taliesin East, it was still growing at the time of his death, twenty years later. For several years he had taken the Fellowship down to

Arizona in the winter months, as Spring Green was generally snowed in for that part of the year. At first he had built a temporary camp in Chandler, Arizona – a series of wood-and-canvas structures only a little more rigid than tents. Then, in 1938, Wright had a little bit of money (for a change) and managed to acquire some 800 acres of land in the Paradise Valley which nobody else seemed to want. He bought the necessary materials – redwood, canvas, rock, cement – and, with the young men of the Fellowship, went to work building one of the most colourful, most romantic groups of buildings erected since the passing of the Mayas.

'Taliesin West is a look over the rim of the world . . . magnificent – beyond words to describe,' Wright wrote. In this beautiful setting, on what he considered to be America's last frontier, Wright built a structure of something he called 'desert concrete' – cement and large chunks of rock, all poured into slanting ramparts – topped with superstructures of redwood and canvas. Through the canvas, light would filter and fill the interior with a lovely glow; just under the deeply cantilevered roof rafters, there would be viewing slots that

34. Kitchen area at Taliesin West. Using the most primitive means and materials, Wright succeeded in creating a magic play of light and shadow, mass and volume. (Photo: Ezra Stoller)

opened up the great desert horizon; and all around the base of the concrete-and-rock parapets, there would be stepped-down terraces, pools, and gardens that made the entire group of buildings a dreamlike oasis in the desert.

The buildings, to start with, contained only the most necessary accommodation for the Fellowship, plus a spacious canvas-topped studio. At the heart of each major structure there was a fireplace of desert concrete, and everywhere was evidence of the materials and the vegetation of the desert. In over-all plan Taliesin West had all the subtlety and delight of Taliesin East – the calculated progression through various kinds of spaces, the sudden surprises, the dramatic building silhouettes, the feeling of oneness with its natural setting. But where Taliesin East seemed a little frilly and, hence, old-fashioned, Taliesin West was a composition of rich and bold forms,

35. Terrace and loggia behind Taliesin West. Wright kept adding to these structures – and changing them around – until his last days. The massive masonry blocks were intended to make a spectacular ruin if and when the wood and canvas superstructure might be gone. (Photo: Ezra Stoller)

36. Living-rooms at Taliesin West. The furniture was designed by Wright. In later years, he was willing to admit that the chairs were not entirely comfortable. (Photo: George Cserna)

shaped by a master sculptor. What ornament there was seemed to emerge from the structure itself – or else from the landscape in terms of planting, lighting, and vistas. Taliesin West was probably influenced by the spirit of Mayan architecture, but it was so original in expression that the Mayas could have provided little more than a point of departure.

A curious fact about Taliesin West (and about some of Wright's houses built near by) was that it seems to be destined to make as fine a ruin as well! For all the perishable materials – wood and canvas – formed a sort of lightweight superstructure on top of the massive ramparts of desert concrete. If this superstructure were ever to be destroyed, the chances are that the ramparts of Taliesin West would remain standing and last forever. Indeed, one of Wright's Arizona houses – the Pauson house in Phoenix, built in 1940 with a core of desert concrete and a superstructure of wood and glass –

burned several years after it was constructed; and the great masonry bulk that survived the fire made a more beautiful silhouette than the house in its entirety had made when it was still standing.

The Usonian houses Wright built during these years represented, in a sense, a modernization of the Prairie house concept. Both in their greater simplicity and in their plan (which took cognizance of the fact that servants had become a vanishing breed), the Usonian houses were realistic and beautiful solutions to living in America in our day. Wright developed several of his Prairie house ideas further: the car-port, the floor slab with integral radiant heating, the built-in furniture, the open kitchen, the utility core, the modular plan, the pinwheel growth of that plan out of a central fireplace, the two-level roof – all these were simplified, modernized, made more economical in construction. But most importantly, perhaps, Wright began to make the Prairie house *look* more modern as well; the Rosenbaum house in Alabama [39], one of the finest Usonian houses built, has the dramatic sweep and simplicity of Mies's Barcelona Pavilion – or possibly of Wright's own unbuilt Yahara Boat Club. The same is true of the Winkler-Goetsch house of the same period – a wood, brick, and glass version of the Barcelona Pavilion in many of its details [40]. It may be argued that Wright did not need Mies to remind him of his early Boat Club project; yet the fact remains that until Wright saw the International Style work in the 1932 exhibition at the Modern Museum, he was well on the way towards forgetting his own magnificently simple projects of the first decade of the century.

In the Usonian houses, Wright laid the foundation for much modern domestic architecture in America during the two decades that followed. These houses were not as dramatic or romantic as Bear Run: but in their modest dignity they solved a problem that needed solving in America, and they solved it to perfection.

Through most of the period between 1910 and 1930 Wright had been receiving the sort of publicity which scandal sheets thrive on: there had been love affairs, murder, fire, foreclosure, courts, and jail. The general public had come to think of him as something of a crackpot, a wild eccentric not to be taken very seriously. In the 1930s all this began to change: Wright's house at Bear Run became the best-known modern house in the world, for pictures of it were published everywhere. Its wild, romantic beauty appealed to everyone, regardless of whether they were familiar with modern architectural theory or not. *Life* published pictures of the Johnson Wax

37. *Light filters into the Taliesin West living-room from different windows and skylights, some of which are of translucent canvas. (Photo: George Cserna)*

38. *View from the loggia joining two wings at Taliesin West. The slanting roof of the living-room is visible at left. (Photo: George Cserna)*

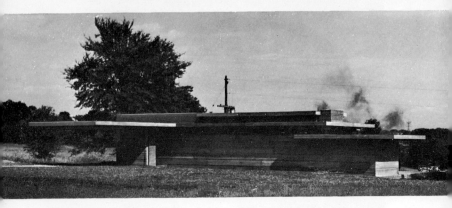

39. Rosenbaum house, Florence, Ala., 1939. One of the most elegant 'Usonian' houses, with sweeping roof planes separated by slots of glass. (Courtesy, Museum of Modern Art)

building on the week of its formal opening, and considered the story so important that the editors gave it the cover and the 'lead' in the issue. In January 1938 the *Architectural Forum*'s editor and publisher, Howard Myers, devoted an entire issue of the magazine to Wright's work. This special issue, virtually designed and written by Wright himself, soon became a collector's item. During the months of preparation of this issue, a close friendship sprang up between Wright and the charming and enthusiastic Myers, and thereafter Wright 'allowed' the *Forum* to publish anything of his that the magazine wanted to print. (In actual fact, this arrangement made it possible for Wright to control closely what was said and written about his work in the professional press, with the result that no really critical evaluation of his work ever appeared in America during his lifetime.) In the same year, 1938, *Life* commissioned Wright to design a small Usonian house for its readers, and this, too, gave Wright's name and work wide and serious currency.

Wright always enjoyed this sort of publicity and became very adept at generating it in his final years. He was an extremely witty and incisive commentator on the passing parade and its various participants, and his sayings became famous everywhere. He soon became a sort of Alexander Woollcott of modern architecture, and,

*40. Winkler-Goetsch house, Okemos, Mich., 1939. Another 'Usonian'
house of tremendous elegance and simplicity. In these houses, Wright –
briefly – became as 'modern' as Mies van der Rohe, in the sense of dropping
all ornament and other complexity. However, his window openings remain
narrowly subdivided. (Courtesy, Museum of Modern Art)*

indeed, Woollcott and Wright were close friends. After Woollcott
first saw the Usonian house for Lloyd Lewis, he wrote to Wright
that he 'told Lloyd that this one makes even a group of *his* friends
look distinguished', a note which Wright cherished. When another
owner of a Usonian house telephoned Wright in desperation because
the rain was pouring in through a leak in the roof, the master calmly
suggested: 'Why don't you move your chair a little bit to one side?'
He told Eliel Saarinen, the late, great Finnish architect, that after he
had seen one of Saarinen's designs, he had thought 'what a great
architect – *I* am!' Wright's magnificent arrogance really blossomed
forth in those years, a delight to him and to all who knew him.
When the late Philadelphia architect George Howe told a fictitious
parable, in which Moses was meant to represent Wright in the latter's
efforts to lead his fellow architects out of bondage, Wright calmly
informed Howe that 'in this story, I am God'. As for his fellow
architects, Wright generously allowed that he admired them all, but,
regrettably, did not feel the same way about their work.

Wright had a good deal of fun making his contemporaries squirm,
and he was entitled to every bit of it. He also lived on a scale far
beyond his means (as he always had), and enjoyed every minute of
buying expensive Japanese prints and Chinese vases, magnificent silk

pyjamas, exquisite ties that must have been specially tailored for him to trail flamboyantly, royal capes of the handsomest tweed available, and so forth. He was generally broke, for he liked to spend whatever he earned as soon as he had earned it. He lived beautifully, tastefully, magnificently. Whenever he came to New York to deliver a short blast, he made an arresting figure striding down Fifth Avenue, pointing out the (to him) most deplorable sights with his elegant cane. As he grew older, he seemed to grow more beautiful also: his flowing silver hair, his erect figure, looking much taller than he really was, his weathered and bronzed face – he put on quite a show. 'Early in life,' he once explained, 'I had to choose between honest arrogance and hypocritical humility. I chose honest arrogance and have seen no occasion to change. . . .'

'No more mantraps; no more landlords. No life imprisoned on shelves of vertical streets, above crowds on gridirons down below. No hard-faced poster façades. . . .' This is how Wright described his project for Broadacre City – the ideal 'living city' developed in the 1930s by the Taliesin Fellowship as a kind of summation of all of Wright's beliefs about how man could exist with dignity in a crowd. From 1934 on, the members of the Fellowship worked on huge models of this ideal city, incorporating various buildings designed by Wright for specific clients and specific needs, but related, by way of underlying principle, to the central themes of his life. Just as everything Corbu designed had some reference to his concept of a Ville Radieuse, first stated by him in the early 1920s, so everything Wright had designed before 1934 (and was to design in later years) was incorporated in the notion of Broadacre City. This, however, is where all similarity ends between Broadacre and the Ville Radieuse.

Where Corbu's city was a collection of vertical towers, free-standing in a park, Wright's city was largely a horizontal expanse, with about an acre of land for each family. It is true that there were a few tall apartment houses also (generally based upon Wright's 1929 project for St Mark's-in-the-Bouwerie), but these towers were really something of an afterthought, and never very clearly related to the rest of the city fabric. In essence, Broadacre was a decentralized, horizontal, close-to-nature city. Indeed, by today's standards it was no city at all; its population densities were those of a village; its economic pattern was that of a self-contained, self-sufficient community of religious or political eccentrics, intent upon showing the rest of humanity how some sort of 'ideal' society could be established on earth; and its functional details were often startling, to say the least – as in a multi-level traffic intersection that seemed about as complicated as a Chinese mousetrap. But despite all its nineteenth-century idealism, despite all its lack of economic and political 'realism' - or perhaps because of all these things – Broadacre City was a marvellously engaging flight of fancy. It was a sort of modern Garden of Eden, complete with vineyards, baths, facilities for physical culture, a circus, stables, and an arboretum. There was an area devoted to 'universal worship', containing – according to Wright's specifications – a 'columbarium, cemetery, nine sectarian temples surrounding a central edifice devoted to universal worship'. There was an establishment housing 'crafts and county architects', and another identified simply as a 'Taliesin equivalent'. In short, Broadacre City was the home of a society devoted to leisure and pleasure, and dominated by the pursuit of the arts. The whole thing was made entirely feasible – in Wright's eyes – because new methods of rapid transportation had annihilated distances. His own contribution to this process of annihilation was a fantastic automobile designed somewhat along the lines of a paddle-wheel steamer, and a helicopter shaped rather like a flying saucer. (Wright was always something of a fanatic about cars: his own favourite automobiles, in later years, were two classic 1940 Lincoln Continentals, painted terracotta red – the Taliesin colour. He had nothing but contempt for most other Detroit models.) Finally, he supplied a design for a petrol station whose pumps were suspended, upside-down, from deep roof overhangs so that cars could be serviced from overhead.

In some respects the notion of Broadacre City was influenced by the teachings of the religious mystic Gurdjieff, whose pupil Mrs Wright had been in Paris before her marriage to Wright. Gurdjieff's beliefs, which Mrs Wright communicated to her husband and to the entire Taliesin Fellowship, were not far removed from Wright's own thoughts about man and nature: they were based upon the conviction that man's life was a simple cycle, originating in the earth and returning to it, and that all artificial interference with this cycle must be avoided. In addition, Gurdjieff believed in the importance of rhythm – music and dance – as a means of bringing body and spirit into harmony, and Mrs Wright, who had always been a dance enthusiast, transmitted her enthusiasms both to her own family and to the Fellowship as a whole. Partly because of these Gurdjieff concepts, Broadacre City became an intensely agrarian sort of place – an agrarian place, that is, replete with facilities for music and dance.

What Wright was really trying to say with Broadacre City is that the modern metropolis, as we know it, should be destroyed and that the only way to save America from 'mobocracy' (his term) was to give everyone enough land and air and light to enable him to live as an individual, rather than a cipher. Wright liked to quote Emerson, who had said that 'cities force growth and make men talkative and entertaining, but they make them artificial'. Wright, though a country boy, was never exactly uncommunicative or dull; but neither was he artificial. Artificiality was the result of living in an unnatural way, Wright thought, and the great, noisy, industrial metropolis was fundamentally unnatural.

We cannot achieve our democratic destiny by mere industrialism, however great [he wrote]. We are by nature gifted as a vast agronomy. In the humane proportion of those two – industrialism and agronomy – we will produce the culture that belongs to Democracy organic. . . .

During the 1930s and 1940s the Communists got the impression that Wright's rejection of the money-centred metropolis, together with his other radical ideas, made him a natural ally. Wright went to Russia in 1937 and reacted to the standard party line and the standard conducted tours in a rather naïve way. He read into some of the plans of the Soviet régime – the development of agricultural centres, for example – a meaning they did not have at all: for Wright's own ideal society was completely *de*centralized, whereas the Stalin state was more centralized than any political organism before or since. Still, the *professed* objectives of the Soviet state – particularly when explained in ways that were likely to appeal to Western idealists – seemed not too far removed from Wright's own, and he developed considerable affection for his hosts. Upon his return to the U.S.A., he had some second thoughts about the role of the individual in a collective society, and decided that his own views were diametrically opposed to those of the Communists. As he told a group of Wisconsin Communists: '[We need] a genuine system of private ownership, a system of capital with its broad base on the ground in the lives of the whole people, instead of standing precariously on its apex for the few. . . .'

None the less, when the Second World War broke out in Europe, Wright again found himself, briefly, on the same side as the Communists. By nature (and because of his special liking for Germany and Japan), Wright became an ardent pacifist – a line the Communists also followed, of course, until the German attack on Russia. Needless to say, Wright's pacifism had nothing to do with any party-political notions; he was opposed to killing human beings and believed that absolute pacifism was the only way to stop wars, just as he thought that absolute Broadacre Cities were the only means of saving individualism. 'War itself,' he once said, 'is a denial of Civilization.' Several members of the Taliesin Fellowship became conscientious objectors, and Wright supported their stand fully. His pacifist position during the war years did not get him into any particular difficulties: everyone by this time expected him to act in unorthodox ways, and, in any case, the popular mood during the Second World War was not very bloodthirsty. After the war was over, and the threat of Soviet power first became apparent to most Americans, Wright again, briefly and naïvely, thought that the way to get along with Stalin's Russia was to be kind to it. He became a sponsor of a cultural conference arranged, in 1948, at the Waldorf-Astoria Hotel in New York between a group of official Soviet 'intellectuals' and a group of fairly notorious American fellow-travellers. That, however, was one of Wright's last major excursions into politics. Except for campaigning for the election of Adlai Stevenson in 1952 and 1956 (partly because he was extremely fond of Stevenson), Wright kept his hands off politics as such. It wasn't that he had been burned; he was simply bored, and thought that most issues as formulated by political parties had nothing to do with the central problems as he saw them – the problems of how to recapture dignity for the individual.

Like other architects not directly involved in the war effort, Wright tried to keep busy, between 1939 and 1945, doing projects that might someday be realized. The most intriguing aspect of these projects is their insistence upon exploring and expanding Wright's notions about plasticity and continuity of space and structure. More and more, Wright got away from straight-lined architecture altogether; his module – if that is the word – became the *circle*, rather than the triangle or polygon; his characteristic vertical form became the outward taper (a narrow base growing into a wider crown, i.e. a kind of tree silhouette); and his favourite structural shape became the spiral or snail. Again and again he would return to these basic themes: in the houses for Herbert Jacobs, Gerald Loeb, and V. C. Morris; in the spa proposed for Elizabeth Arden; in the great laboratory tower for the Johnson Wax building; in the drive-in laundry for Benjamin Adelman; and in the fantastic multi-saucer country club proposed for Huntington Hartford (and meant to be placed on top of one of the Hollywood hills), Wright made the never-ending circle and the outward taper his central themes.

41. Friedman house, Pleasantville, N.Y., 1950. A house based on a circular theme, rising like a small fortress out of its hilltop. (Photo: Ezra Stoller)

Most of these projects were never built; but the circle pattern remained in Wright's work and dominated it throughout his final years. Indeed, his feelings against the square as a harsh, inhuman, artificial thing became so strong that he actually laid out whole developments for Kalamazoo, Michigan, and Pleasantville, New York, in which the individual building lots were circular plots, one acre in size. It was never very clearly explained what was to happen to (and who was to own) the space *between* the circles – the part of the Swiss cheese that isn't holes – but Wright was never very much concerned with problems of this sort, which, he felt, were the creation of book-keepers and others of their ilk. It seemed to him that no one who had any love for landscape could ever impose a rectilinear, geometric pattern upon the face of the earth, as such a pattern was fundamentally alien to nature. (Wright, incidentally, had gone in for contour ploughing at Spring Green long before this became accepted farming practice in the United States!)

The spiral was the next logical step; it is the circle brought into the third and fourth dimensions. One of the first spiral structures proposed by Wright was the (unbuilt) planetarium project for

Gordon Strong, done in 1925. Strong had come to Wright wanting nothing more than a place from which to gaze at the skies; by the time Wright was through, he had redesigned all of Sugar Loaf Mountain, in Maryland, by turning its top into a kind of broad corkscrew shape providing a spiral motor approach to the planetarium on top. (Wright was a perfectly good driver, but some of his notions of traffic patterns were, to say the least, eccentric.)

From the planetarium project on, Wright kept coming back to the idea of the snail shape until, during the later war years, he developed two projects in which the spiral ramp became the central theme: the San Francisco store for V. C. Morris, and the New York museum for the Solomon Guggenheim Foundation. Both were built after the war.

The Morris store [42] is really a remodelling job, though this is hardly evident: for if anything at all remained of the original building, Wright managed to conceal it completely. In a sense the store is two kinds of architecture: a remarkable façade, and an equally remarkable interior space. The façade is simply a blank wall of brick – no show windows whatever – penetrated by a single bold arch, very much like a façade by H. H. Richardson translated from stone to brick. The trick, of course, was to make the store front inviting by making it mysterious and quite different from any other store front in any other street or city: as, from the sidewalk, you can see none of the vases, candlesticks, and other accessories for sale inside, you are irresistibly drawn into this strange store that refuses to advertise its wares. In a sense Wright had taken a leaf from those ancient shops in St James's Street whose owners believe in leaving the windows murky and the displays decrepit. It works like a charm.

Inside, however, there is no trace of Richardson whatever. Here the entire space is filled with a lovely two-storey spiral ramp curling up gracefully towards a huge, circular glass dome that fills the store with light. Everywhere the details are in harmony with the circle theme: tables are circular, as are lighting fixtures, suspended planting trays, stools, and the glass bowls that make up the great skylight. The whole thing has a unity and strength rarely seen in a building, and a poetic loveliness that makes up many times over for the fact that, as a sales machine, the store probably is not as efficient as it might have been. But the most extraordinary thing that happens in this space is the tangible movement in evidence everywhere: as you

walk down the graceful spiral ramp, you become strangely uncon-
scious of your own movement; instead, the space itself seems to be
slowly revolving around you. There may be some potential buyers
who have been discouraged by this strange sensation; but most
visitors to the store undoubtedly sense that here, in this little
'unimportant' gem of a building, Frank Lloyd Wright added a new
dimension to space.

In the Morris store Wright used the ramp simply as a means of
getting from the street floor to the mezzanine level. There are only
token displays on the ramp itself. But in the Guggenheim Museum
[43–5 and frontispiece], he made the ramp the actual gallery space,
and paintings are supposed to be hung on the spiralling walls. The
spiral ramp makes five complete turns around a central circular well;

*42. Morris store, San Francisco, Calif., 1948. A spiral-ramp structure – the
first of its kind actually built by Wright – under a glass dome. As the visitor
ascends on the ramp, the space around him seems to revolve gently and take
on an infinite number of changing aspects. (Photo: Maynard Parker)*

as it makes these turns, the spiral becomes slightly wider, so that the form of the building tapers outward in the characteristic Wrightian fashion. The light for this great circular well comes from two sources: from a large skylight dome above, and from strips of glass above the spiralling walls which follow the curvature of the structure all the way to the top. 'They're going to try and figure this one out for years to come,' Wright would say with glee as the Museum went up on Fifth Avenue.

In many curious ways the Guggenheim snail resembles the main entrance hall to the museums of the Vatican in Rome, which was built some twenty years earlier. But the Vatican spiral hall (though also skylit through a glass dome) is used only as a means of getting visitors upstairs and down, whereas the Guggenheim snail was meant to be the museum itself. In rationalizing this form, Wright made three points: firstly, that the slow descent would help visitors avoid 'museum fatigue' (they are carried upstairs in an elevator); secondly, that the outward-slanting walls of the spiral ramp resembled easels and thus permitted a more faithful presentation of paintings than vertical walls would; and, thirdly, that 'the rectilinear frame of reference in a painting', as the *Architectural Forum* put it, 'has more to do with the frame than with the painting'.

Now, with all due respect (indeed with supreme respect) for Wright, this is unmitigated nonsense. The Guggenheim Museum is almost impossible as a museum in the normal sense: if it had not been for certain changes made after Wright's death, a gallery-goer would have had to stand on an incline, look at a wall sloping away from him – a wall, moreover, that is curved so that any *large* paintings would have had to be fitted to its contours – and, while doing all this, he would have had to avoid being blinded by a continuous band of light from above, which appears aimed directly at his eyes! It is probably untrue to say, as one ex-Taliesin man suggested, that Wright hated the paintings in the Guggenheim collection and built a building to destroy them. He *did* dislike most modern art and had very little knowledge of or interest in it. But the chances are that the Guggenheim Collection was far too unimportant to him to try to demolish it in such an elaborate manner. The fact is, quite simply, that Wright just *had* to build one great, wonderful spiral before he died, and he managed to sell the Guggenheim Foundation on the idea that it would make a good museum. (In 1947 he tried to sell Edgar Kaufmann, the Pittsburgh department store owner and client

43. *Guggenheim Museum, New York City, completed in 1959. This is the view from the downtown end of Fifth Avenue. The big spiral in the foreground contains the galleries; the smaller, circular structure to the rear contains administrative offices. (Photo: George Cserna)*

44. *A circular auditorium is located in the basement of the Guggenheim Museum. Its form and its low ceiling-height make it an ideal room for smaller meetings. (Photo: George Cserna)*

for 'Falling Water', on the idea of building a spiral parking garage in downtown Pittsburgh – and later in the great Pittsburgh Point project. This suggestion made a good deal more sense than using the spiral for a museum gallery, although the parking attendants would have had to get their schooling in a hamster cage.) In short, the Guggenheim Foundation got a fabulous piece of architectural sculpture – the only completed work of uncompromising plasticity and continuity achieved by Wright – and should now make plans to build a place in which to show its paintings.

In several respects the Guggenheim Museum is an extension of earlier Wright buildings. When compared with the Larkin building of 1904, for example, it becomes quite clear what Wright had been driving at over the years. The Larkin building is really the Guggenheim Museum done in rectangular geometry: it has the same central well (but the well is a rectangle); it has galleries overlooking the well (but the galleries are level floors); it has a great skylight illuminating

45. Dome above Guggenheim galleries. The reverse curve of the spiral ramp clears a circular lift shaft and, incidentally, provides a visual point of reference for visitors ascending or descending the ramp. (Photo: George Cserna)

46. *Chapel at Florida Southern College, Lakeland, Fla., 1940. The folded planes that form this hexagonal structure are part of Wright's attempt to get away from boxlike architecture. The resulting forms are remarkably similar to those of Froebelian games, on which Wright was brought up in his childhood. (Photo: Ezra Stoller)*

the well (but the skylight, again, is rectangular); and it has a simple, over-all form with stair towers, etc., pushed out beyond the central mass (but the form is squared off, as are the stair towers). In short, the road from Larkin to Guggenheim is the great avenue of Wright's creative development over half a century – from an architecture that was monumentally simple (but still boxlike) to an architecture that was fluid, plastic, continuous, and has utterly changed our ideas of the nature of space and structure. In between these two great buildings there were many others that are milestones along the way: Unity Church in 1906, with its great skylit space of many levels;

121

Johnson Wax of 1936, with its fluid forms, its glass roof, and its mezzanines; and the Florida Southern College buildings from 1938 onwards, with their suggestion of *folded* planes *à la* Froebel, their many surprising levels, their astonishing play of light from above [46].

The Guggenheim Museum was almost finished when Wright died in April 1959. Apart from its importance as a plastic statement, it is important as Wright's last slap at the city. No building could be designed to fit less well into the established urban pattern – and that, in Wright's view, was about as great a compliment as you could pay a building. Both in form and in its clay colour the Guggenheim Museum looks like a growing organism in a graveyard – not pretty, but certainly alive and kicking. Its exterior is perhaps a little too plain and crudely finished – one of the few *un*ornamented Wright buildings – perhaps because Wright wanted nothing to distract from the boldness of the principal statement. But the chances are that when the planting begins to trail over the curved parapets, the Guggenheim Museum may look a good deal softer than it did on its opening day – almost mellow towards its surroundings, as its creator grew to be towards *his* surroundings in the last days of his life.

47. Project for a parking garage, Pittsburgh, Pa., 1947. Here the spiral ramp was used to solve an eminently practical problem. This project was designed while the Guggenheim Museum was on the drawing-boards. (Courtesy, Taliesin Fellowship)

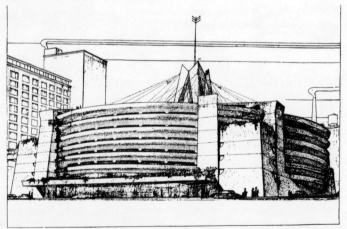

FIFTEEN

Like Le Corbusier and Mies van der Rohe, Wright had more work after the Second World War than he had ever had before. In addition to the Guggenheim, the Johnson Wax tower was built; the Florida Southern College campus at Lakeland progressed at a rapid pace – the sixteenth building nearing completion at the time of Wright's death; in Bartlesville, Oklahoma, Wright at long last found a client who was willing to build the tower originally designed in 1929 for St Mark's-in-the-Bouwerie; and all over the country there were new houses, big and small.

In addition, Wright worked on a vast number of projects that never went beyond the paper stage. Like Le Corbusier, he produced a seemingly endless flow of these detailed studies. One reason was that he was willing to jump into any situation that seemed even

48. Project for a country club in the Hollywood hills, Calif., 1947. Saucer-shaped platforms were to have been cantilevered out from a mountain-top to carry restaurants, tennis courts, etc. (Courtesy, Taliesin Fellowship)

123

faintly promising, to get his foot into the smallest crack in any door; another was that his students at Taliesin represented a large enthusiastic (and cheap) labour force, delighted to try anything that might advance the cause of organic architecture. Among the most impressive studies of the post-war years was the country club for Huntington Hartford mentioned earlier – a jagged pyramid of stone growing out of a mountain-top, with half a dozen circular concrete saucers or trays cantilevered from the central mass of rock to carry restaurants, gardens, and pools half-way between Hollywood and heaven [48]. There was a towerlike hotel for Dallas, sheathed in magnesium and glass, and tapered outward in the characteristic tree silhouette. (Unfortunately, the client died before the project could go ahead.) There was the plan to develop one of the most dramatic sites in the U.S. – the Pittsburgh Point Park, the triangular tip of the city formed by the Allegheny and Monongahela rivers. This study was financed by a group of prominent Pittsburgh businessmen under the leadership of Edgar Kaufmann, but unfortunately came to nothing; instead, several real-estate promoters perpetrated an act of singular architectural barbarism on this beautiful site, and a great opportunity was lost.

As Wright passed his eightieth birthday and approached the age of ninety, he became, if anything, more rather than less prolific. The tower in Bartlesville for the H. C. Price Co. [49–51] was completed in 1956 – an eighteen-storey structure containing both offices and apartments, and making up for a rather impractical layout by its success in turning a multicellular building into a statement of individualism (rather than a giant file cabinet). In 1955 Wright's occasional home town of Madison, Wisconsin, voted for him to design a magnificent civic centre on Lake Monona. (The project – an extravaganza of circles and ramps – was shelved because local politicians were afraid of its cost.) In 1957 Wright heard that the State of Arizona was about to put up a new State Capitol building. Preliminary plans showed that the proposed structure would be just another 'box', looking like the head office for a drugstore chain, rather than a centre of democratic government. Wright decided that there was

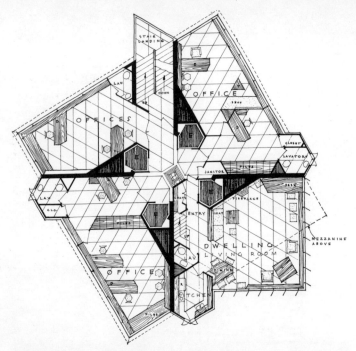

50. Plan of typical floor in Price tower, showing the cross-shaped 'spine' that supports the building. All floors were cantilevered out from this 'spine'. (Courtesy, Taliesin Fellowship)

still a chance to prevent this particular act of official idiocy, and submitted a proposal of his own: a huge, romantic, tepee-shaped structure of hexagonal concrete grilles ('a vast lath house', Wright called it), surrounded by lower structures, gardens, fountains, and easy pedestrian approaches. (He felt that a seat of government deserved a more leisurely and dignified approach than that suggested by a limousine tearing down a six-lane highway.) Despite a great deal of public agitation on behalf of Wright's lovely design, there was no stopping the bureaucrats, and the drugstore box was built instead. Finally, in that same year, Wright began work on a fantastic project for King Feisal II of Iraq – a fabulous opera house and civic auditorium for Baghdad, to be located on an island in the middle of the Tigris River. (While he was working on that design, he decided that he might as well also create the new University of Baghdad, although that commission had been given to Walter Gropius.) Wright's cultural centre was to have been a circular structure, rather like a big musical top; it would have been approached by means of a spiral-ramp highway leading up to the central complex, and guaranteed to chill the blood of any but the most experienced motorists. The building itself was to have been topped off by a glass-and-gold spire, which Wright referred to as 'Aladdin's Wonderful Lamp'. And the whole thing would, indeed, have made Haroun Al-Rashid (or any of his Victorian admirers) goggle-eyed. Unfortunately, the revolution in Iraq and the murder of young King Feisal put an end to this project as well.

Meanwhile Wright received many honours, in the U.S.A. as well as abroad: the City of Florence awarded him its Gold Medal in 1951, and Wright (who had in earlier years said some unkind things about the classicism of the Renaissance) allowed that the great architects of that period in Florence did, after all, seem to have known what

51. Entrance area in Price tower. Every detail, including the light fixtures, was designed to relate to the triangular module of the structure. (Photo: George Cserna)

they were doing. However, he also felt, upon seeing his work exhibited in one of the great Florentine *palazzi*, that he did not have to
worry about the judgement of history. Two years before the Florentine medal, in 1949, the American Institute of Architects had, rather
belatedly, decided to award him *its* Gold Medal – only to detract
from that honour a few years later by naming one of its 'safe',
conservative members the 'Architect of the Century' (the century in
question being the one dominated, for more than half its span, by
Wright's genius). Wright's own reaction to these honours was pre-
dictably sarcastic: what really worried him was that he seemed to be
becoming acceptable and even fashionable – a terrible fate for *any*
radical! To keep the opposition opposed, Wright made a point of
being outrageous in public as often as he could. His public pronouncements on such matters as the modern metropolis, the International Style, modern art, cigarettes, automobiles, clothes, TV

*52. Walker house, Carmel, Calif., 1952. The house sits on a promontory
overlooking the Pacific Ocean. (Photo: Ezra Stoller)*

commercials, Washington, D.C., and on all other architects became increasingly biting. He discovered that one way of making people sit up and take notice of what he had to say was to start by dropping a bombshell or two, and then to talk quietly (and often sensibly) in the ensuing silence. This is, of course, one of the accepted techniques employed by publicists of every stripe, and it contains certain dangers: for example, Wright occasionally produced designs that were so fantastic as to border on the preposterous – simply because he seemed to feel that this was an effective way of making a point. His 1956 Mile High building for Chicago's lake front was an example of this; if this giant needle-shaped tower with its 130,000 daytime inhabitants had ever been built, the problems of moving people, supplies, and services in and out of the structure would have been insoluble without razing the entire centre of Chicago (which was, of course, precisely what Wright had had in mind).

This sort of thing hardly endeared Wright to his more 'practical' fellow men, and it is probably for this reason that Wright was denied so many important commissions during the last years of his life. It is none the less unforgivable that the U.S. government never awarded a single commission to Wright, while lesser architects were asked to design new American embassies, consulates, military academies, post offices, and memorials all over the world. It is just as unforgivable that the states of Wisconsin and Arizona never awarded a commission to their illustrious citizen. And it is deplorable indeed that the American Institute of Architects, which often forms committees to recommend men for important public commissions, did not once remember its own Gold Medallist of 1949. Admittedly, Wright did not make it easy for bureaucrats to approach him; but, then, no one ever really made the effort. The result, in any case, is that the various governments of the U.S. do not possess a single building by America's most creative architect!

Wright never seemed to grow old. When he celebrated his eightieth birthday, he talked about moving farther out into the Arizona desert in ten years or so because the lights and telegraph lines of civilization were beginning to intrude upon the views from Taliesin West. Whenever he came to New York to stay in his (Wright-decorated) red-and-gold suite at the Hotel Plaza – from which he supervised the construction of the Guggenheim Museum – he seemed easily as spry as any of the bellboys, and a great deal more alert. And on the rare occasions when his work was exhibited next to that of younger men, he generally made his juniors look rather timid and stuffy by comparison with his own daring flamboyance.

Because he *was* the great Patriarch of architecture, no one ever really challenged him, however outrageous he might appear in some of his pronouncements. Le Corbusier and Mies van der Rohe might be 'Corbu' and 'Mies' to every architect the world over, but Wright was always 'Mr Wright'. He was the King – unchallenged, unchallengeable. At times, when he was staying at the Plaza (which he considered to be the Royal Residence in New York), he would take friends on a tour of the building, calmly walking into board meetings and similar gatherings in the hotel's private rooms and interrupting the proceedings to point out (with his malacca cane) a decorative detail here or a flaw there. It never occurred to anyone to stop him: his presence was far too commanding. On TV and radio programmes to which he had been invited as a guest, he would soon take over and run the show, and the cameras and microphones seemed irresistibly drawn to his face and voice as if by some sort of magnetic force. All of this Wright found exceedingly pleasant; indeed, one of his favourite stories in later years was about a lady who had asked Adlai Stevenson whether all the public adulation to which he was subjected was doing him any harm. 'Adlai answered that it was all right so long as he didn't inhale,' Wright would recall, grinning wickedly.

As a matter of fact, Wright inhaled deeply and with great satisfaction. After all, this was the pay-off, in a small way, for the poverty and the early struggle, for the condescension towards the country hick in Sullivan's office, for the innumerable projects left unbuilt and derided, for the years of yellow-journalist persecution, for the meanness of his fellow professionals and the grudging slowness of their recognition. Still, though he did enjoy the honours that came his way late in life, he managed to do so without any loss of dignity. To some he even seemed to grow rather mellow: when the National Institute of Arts and Letters awarded its Gold Medal to him in 1953, he stated, in mock alarm, that 'a shadow falls . . . I feel coming on me a strange disease – humility'. But the bitterness over much of the past was never far below the surface. 'Although all may raise the flowers now, none have become trees,' he wrote to a friend shortly before he died.

Why so late and why never the least gratitude from those who took heed? As the years have rolled by I have come to believe that architects themselves are really all that is the matter with Architecture. . . . Well, let's start again at scratch: found a liberal society for the life of Architecture, for the lovers of good, organic Architecture. *Architecture* this time first, not architects. . . . More of this later.

Alas, his time was up; a few weeks later, in Phoenix, Arizona, on 9 April 1959, Frank Lloyd Wright died after a minor operation. According to the records, he was just two months short of ninety. With him, something important in America died also.

He was buried in Spring Green, at Taliesin; his coffin was carried on a farm cart. Before long, a chapel designed by Wright in his last years will be completed at Taliesin, and his remains will be transferred to this final burial place.

53. Taliesin, Spring Green, Wis. Here, among the hills where he was born, Wright was buried in the spring of 1959.

A week before his death, Frank Lloyd Wright gave one of his regular informal talks to the Taliesin Fellowship.

What is fundamental to the architect-at-heart [he asked]? What is it he must have? He has to have health, he has to have strength – strength of character most of all – strength of mind, strength of muscle. He has to know life, and he has to know life by studying it. And how do you proceed to study life most successfully and directly? By living it. To live the life . . . means the study primarily of Nature. . . . Yours is the opportunity to shape and to determine the shape of things to come. You are the shape-hewers and the shape-knowers, or you are not architects at heart. But it takes a long time to make that kind of an architect. . . .

Strength, character, life, heart: it took most of a century to complete the work of Frank Lloyd Wright; and when his work was done, architecture had given mankind a new promise of civilization.

FURTHER READING

The basic book on Frank Lloyd Wright is *An Autobiography* by Frank Lloyd Wright (Duell, Sloan & Pearce, New York) and to it should be added his last work: *A Testament* by Frank Lloyd Wright (Horizon Press Inc., New York).

Collected essays and lectures will be found, well illustrated, in *The Future of Architecture* and *An American Architecture,* both of which are also published by the Horizon Press Inc.

Wright's output of buildings and drawings is covered in detail in only two books: *In the Nature of Materials: the Buildings of Frank Lloyd Wright 1887–1941* by Henry-Russell Hitchcock (Duell, Sloan & Pearce) and *The Drawings of Frank Lloyd Wright* by Arthur Drexler (Horizon Press Inc.), but his more recent buildings have not yet been collected comprehensively in any book.

The only available biography of Wright to date is the sensational *Frank Lloyd Wright – a biography* by Finis Farr (Charles Scribner's Sons, New York) which contains some information Wright himself did not care to mention in the autobiography, but which is very weak on the architecture.

Interpretations and evaluations of Wright and his work are found in all the standard histories of modern architecture, but one should also note *Frank Lloyd Wright* by Vincent J. Scully (Masters of World Architecture series, George Braziller Inc., New York) for a highly original attempt to place Wright in the context of architectural history.

A discriminating selection of Wright's writings and buildings has been put together by Edgar Kaufmann and Ben Raeburn. The book – *Frank Lloyd Wright: Writings and Buildings* – is available in hard covers and as a paperback (Horizon Press Inc.). Other paperbacks on Wright's work are *The Future of Architecture, The Natural House,* and *The Living City* (all published by New American Library, New York).

INDEX

Italic numbers refer to illustrations

Some other Pelicans on architecture are described on the following pages

ALSO BY PETER BLAKE

MIES VAN DER ROHE

Among the great personalities who have pioneered this century's revolution in building, Mies van der Rohe, for twenty years director of
architecture at the Illinois Institute of Technology, is the least theoretical, the most practical, and in many ways the most inspired. The son
of a simple mason in Germany, he served an apprenticeship amid the
dirt and noise of building sites. He comprehends materials perfectly,
from the modest brick to the marble and onyx of his famous Barcelona
Pavilion or the expanses of glass on the magnificent bronze-tinted
Seagram Building in New York. For him structure is an overriding
principle.

'I don't want to be interesting' he once stated. 'I want to be good.'
Nevertheless it is impossible not to be interested by the career of this
most professional of architects, with his severe classical standards and
his ability to throw off such intriguing principles as 'Less is more.'

This study by a distinguished American architect is taken from
The Master Builders, described by Sir Herbert Read as 'a perceptive
and exciting book.'

Also available: LE CORBUSIER

AN INTRODUCTION TO MODERN
ARCHITECTURE

J. M. RICHARDS

An Introduction to Modern Architecture, which has been newly revised and brought up to date, sets out to explain what 'modern' architecture is all about. In these days, when the need for new buildings is so great and so many building plans are being made, it is specially important that everyone should have an understanding of the principles of architecture, and the author, disapproving of the treatment of architecture as a professional mystery or merely a matter of correct taste, asks (and tries to answer) the simple question: 'Conventions and habits apart, what sort of architecture does our time really require?'

With the help of gravure illustrations, as well as line drawings, he explains how modern buildings come to look as they do, discussing the technical practices and the changing needs and ideals on which modern architects' work is based. Also, believing that architecture can only be explained as part of a continuous growth, he shows modern architecture against the background out of which it grew, giving an outline history of the struggle to produce a sane architecture which has been going on throughout the past hundred years.

THE FUTURE OF LONDON

EDWARD CARTER

The Future of London is unique among town-planning books. It is both exciting to read and authoritative in content. It shows vividly that the factors underlying any plan – land-values, traffic, housing and social facilities, open spaces, skyscrapers, and the aesthetic quality of what is built – are something of vital concern to every city dweller, for they will determine the pattern of his life in the future.

A city is not just a mass of concrete, steel, bricks, and asphalt. It is also a place where thousands or millions of people are born and brought up, work and play, grow old and die. A modern capital must provide the conditions in which its inhabitants can lead full, happy, and healthy lives.

In this fascinating discussion of the decay and renewal of the Metropolis, the Director of the Architectural Association looks at the different plans, past and present, that exist for its development. He shows that the need for action is urgent, for with every year of unplanned chaos the problems grow more intractable.

It is for us to decide whether tomorrow's London will be an uninhabitable jungle or a capital to be proud of.

AN OUTLINE OF EUROPEAN
ARCHITECTURE

NIKOLAUS PEVSNER

This is a history of Western architecture as an expression of Western civilization, described in its growth from the ninth to the twentieth century. It tells the story of architecture through the medium of its outstanding expressions in actual building. The method adopted is to discuss a few representative buildings of each period and country in some detail and to avoid dull cataloguing. The aim of the book is to make readers appreciate architectural values. It is written for reading, not merely for reference, and it makes interesting reading indeed in its concentration and its combination of warmth and scholarship.

This famous book is now available in a seventh edition which has been considerably revised and extended. Increased in format, the book now contains over 300 excellent illustrations.

Professor Pevsner is head of the Department of the History of Art, Birkbeck College, University of London. He edits the Pelican History of Art and Architecture.